Language Development

Language Development

Circle Time Sessions to Improve Communication Skills

Marion Nash

with Jackie Lowe and Tracey Palmer

David Fulton Publishers

London

David Fulton Publishers Ltd
The Chiswick Centre, 414 Chiswick High Road, London W4 5TF

www.fultonpublishers.co.uk

First published in Great Britain by David Fulton Publishers 2002

Note: The right of Marion Nash, Jackie Lowe and Tracey Palmer to be identified as the authors of this work has been asserted by them in accordance with the Copyright, Designs and Patents Act 1988.

Copyright © Marion Nash, Jackie Lowe and Tracey Palmer 2002

British Library Cataloguing in Publication Data
A catalogue record for this book is available from the British Library

ISBN 1–85346–879–7

Typeset by FiSH Books, London
Printed in Great Britain by Bell & Bain Ltd, Glasgow

Contents

To Tom, with love

So much that I value has been added by Tom's energy,
enthusiasm and chuckles.

Foreword

'I'm afraid I can't put it more clearly . . .
for I can't understand it myself to begin with'

Although they remain true for many children today, Alice spoke these words in a much more leisurely age when there was time to ponder and consider before speaking. Today's 'rapid response' world demands that we all live at an altogether faster pace, and the ability to think and respond quickly and to develop the linguistic skills associated with verbal agility are more important than ever before. Our communication systems are now global and the telecommunication and computer technology that has made this possible places unprecedented linguistic demands upon the citizens who live in this new culture. Those of us who are unable to communicate effectively suffer not only the pain of unmet personal needs but also the bleak loneliness of cultural exclusion. 'To put it simply, culture is about "shared meanings". Now, language is the privileged medium in which we "make sense" of things, in which meaning is produced and exchanged. Meanings can only be shared through our common access to language' (Hall 1997).

This change of pace is reflected in the culture of the modern classroom, and children who lack an expressive vocabulary which can be used to define and articulate their opinions, feelings and knowledge are crucially handicapped in all aspects of their lives within and outside of the school environment. For such children, prompt and appropriate intervention is of paramount importance if they are not to be consigned to years of debilitating frustration and muffled hopelessness. Appropriate intervention entails two activities. First we must clearly and, as accurately as possible, define and understand what the problem is. This is of primary importance because it informs the second activity, which is to devise and institute suitable teaching and learning strategies, which will provide children with the assistance they so desperately need. For the chosen strategies to be effective they must take into account not only the needs of the particular child but, also, the limitations imposed by the larger scenario of the school environment. These include staffing issues, the availability of time, curriculum demands and organisational issues. All of these factors need to be understood and accounted for if children who are identified as academically vulnerable are to benefit from their time at school.

Marion, Jackie and Tracey have worked together as a team to produce this invaluable set of materials. Because they work in different professional capacities they have each been able to contribute something special to the book, which is a synthesis of their combined expertise, experience and theoretical knowledge. Through their collaboration they have achieved a book that addresses each link in the chain of imperatives listed above and have produced a thorough, well researched and pragmatic set of materials which encompass all of the various skills needed to develop language, thinking skills and the effective exchange of ideas, and which have the added benefit of harnessing each child's strengths through a clear understanding of the different learning styles described by Howard Gardner.

Marion Nash's interest in the dynamics of group work began when she researched her master's degree in 1989 and she has continued to research, hone and refine her ideas as an educational psychologist in Plymouth. Her precise knowledge of the problems which individual children can encounter as they grow up and her awareness of the importance of offering activities which raise confidence and build self-esteem imbue this book.

Jackie Lowe is a speech and language therapist and has been able to contribute technical expertise to the continuum of concepts which children need to grasp if they are to learn, think and communicate effectively. Tracey Palmer is a teacher and is, therefore, fully aware of what is and what is not practicable within the school environment. This is an essential contribution because a unified approach by all staff and a vigorous commitment to the same objectives, and the procedures that are chosen to accomplish them, is probably the single most important factor that will predict the success or failure of any scheme of work.

The intervention programme offered in this book is underscored by the belief that the teacher can play a vital role in mediating the curriculum to prevent manifestations of unease and fear of failure that can so easily disrupt learning in children who suffer from destructively low self-esteem. The intervention programme is designed to begin at the first possible opportunity and the importance of positive feedback is frequently restated throughout the session plans. Reaching beyond purely academic targets, each session is designed to offer children the joy of personal empowerment that proceeds from the knowledge that they are being guided, via tasks that are just challenging enough to offer the satisfaction of success, toward increasing independence safe in the knowledge that all their efforts will be valued and praised.

The modern classroom with its government-driven focus on academic achievement can be an alarming place for the linguistically vulnerable child, and groups like the ones advocated here can provide a sanctuary for those children who need time to untangle confused thoughts and who can only do so in a setting that offers diverse opportunities, time to ponder and, most importantly, the absence of pressure.

The intervention programme offered by this book provides continuity and progression from the nursery class till well into Key Stage 2. By intervening at the earliest opportunity it seeks to prevent the destructive downward spiral whereby the struggling child is driven by their sense of failure to resort to acting out in a symbolic way and becomes, in time, a child with school-related behavioural problems. Each session is well structured, combining moments of quiet and calm with activities that are lively and full of fun. The materials required for these activities are readily available in all schools and are supported by a bank of photocopiable resources supplied by the authors.

For many years, in the Quality Circle Time model I have advocated that schools should consider setting up 'Circles of Support' alongside the timetabled weekly circle meetings for all pupils (Mosley 1988, 1991). A circle of support is a smaller, more specifically focused meeting for children who have been identified as having needs that are beyond the remit of the larger circle groups which cater for around 30 pupils. These support circles are therapeutic because they are more specific, and have two adults who work together and can sustain one another so that they have sufficient energy to make available the extra large portions of empathy, warmth and genuineness that some children need (Rogers 1959). My team and I have always promoted the setting up of this type of group for children whose levels of emotional disrepair are greater than the typical. It is therefore very exciting to celebrate the innovative work of Marion and her team to successfully support children who have specific language difficulties.

Jenny Mosley, July 2002
Director of the Whole School Quality Circle Time Model

Jenny Mosley Consultancies,
28a Gloucester Road,
Trowbridge,
Wiltshire BA14 0AA
www.circle-time.co.uk

References

Carroll, L. (2000) *Alice's Adventures in Wonderland*. London: Bloomsbury Publishing, p. 55.

Hall, S. (1997) *Representation: Cultural Representation and Signifying Practices*. London: Sage Publications, p.1

Mosley, J. (1988) Some Implications Arising from a Small-scale Study of a Circle-based Programme Initiated for the Tutorial Period. *Pastoral Care*, June.

Mosley, J. (1991) An Evaluative Account of the Working of a Peer Support Group within a Comprehensive School. *Support for Learning* 6(4).

Rogers, C. (1959) Client Centred Therapy. Boston, MA: Houghton Mifflin.

Acknowledgements

The publication of this book has been made possible by the foresight and support of the people who work in Plymouth Education Authority and those who direct it. The work has been supported and encouraged by Sohail Faruqi, Director for Lifelong Learning, and Bronwen Lacey, Head of Service (Learner Support), in line with their commitment to enrich the educational experiences of children in the City of Plymouth. As a result many children in other areas will have the opportunity to grow in confidence and develop new skills through working with the materials.

Ford Primary School in Plymouth is at the heart of the development of this book. Many thanks to the head, staff, governors and parents of Ford Primary School and Nursery Unit, and particularly the children who were the initial inspiration for the work. Special thanks are due to the head of the school for his support and foresight. Many thanks to June Spanner, whose enthusiastic support of the groups has been much appreciated, and Val Galer, who continues the important work of running the groups. Thanks too to the teaching assistants who pioneered the running of the groups in schools, the admin team and Mary McGill, chair of governors, for her interest and enthusiasm.

Thanks to Andrew Burnett and Narelle for their two super ideas. Thanks too to the schools and nurseries for the enthusiastic support for the groupwork, Mary McNaughton for professional input and support, and Claire Easterbrook for her much valued involvement.

Special thanks to my colleague Mel Ainscow whose support and interest has been much appreciated.

Thanks too to Jude Bowen at David Fulton for her support and guidance in my first publication and to Jenny Mosley, whose work and energy I have always admired. This book could not have been written without the support and foresight of Maggie Carter, Principal Educational Psychologist. Thanks also to Mick Johnson, Colin Moore, Peter Jones, Ellen Wright and all my educational psychologist colleagues.

Special thanks are due to the administration team, especially to Pamela who took on the formatting of the material so creatively, and Liz whose support and technical skills were much appreciated. Many, many thanks Angie, Thomas and George who have shared the excitement and the trials. Especial thanks to you Angie for your technical support.

Thanks to my friends for their readiness to listen and to Heidi Lowe for her lovely drawings.

This book contains many traditional and tried and true materials and if I have omitted to attribute materials to people it is not intentional and I hereby take this opportunity to thank them.

Marion Nash, Educational Psychologist

Introduction: How Circle Time Has Been Developed in Schools over Time

> Hearts, mind and hand interact with language and make learning possible.
>
> (Philip Taylor, 1985)

Circle Time groupwork is a key strategy which has been used successfully in schools for many years to give children opportunities to develop a range of vital social and academic skills. Circlework can be of great benefit to children who have assumed a passive or inattentive role in class rather than taking the personal risks involved in putting forward their ideas, perceptions and questions in the public arena. The feelings of support and safety created within the group can encourage the learner to take the first few steps towards contributing in class.

In order to develop both cooperative circlework and emotional awareness, Leslie Button used developmental groupwork as active tutorial work in secondary schools in the 1960s. Later it was realised that the safe and creative ethos in which the activities were set would be just as productive for the younger child. Through the work of educational practitioners the idea of sessions incorporating developmental groupwork was developed in the educational field as Circle Time. Jenny Mosley was one of the first practitioners to develop and apply a whole-school quality Circle Time model in British schools in the early 1980s and her work had a tremendous positive impact on schools, teachers and children. Jenny has always made a strong case for spending quality time on Circle Time because of the wide-ranging positive effects it has on pupils' listening and speaking skills and wider personal, social and academic achievement.

Jenny has continued to develop ideas based on this very positive model and has always included consideration of the needs of the adults who support the pupils, making Circle Time a very powerful and enjoyable and inclusive way to develop self-esteem and communication skills. Jenny's enthusiastic presentations have inspired many to adopt this approach in their schools, with many attendant benefits.

One of my early encounters with whole-school circlework was in 1989. I was researching for my master's degree based on a study of a middle school which used developmental groupwork throughout the school. I was impressed with the children's skills in communication and language. They were especially skilled in using language to resolve conflict and to work together effectively, and my thesis reflected this. I came to Plymouth in 1990 to join the educational psychology team and I worked over a ten-year period to raise awareness of the special ethos and benefits of Circle Time with many headteachers, teaching staff, assistants, speech and language therapists and parents. Part of my work was to train professionals in the skills they would need to develop Circle Time in schools. As part of this development with schools I found Jenny's books, especially *Turn Your School Round* and *Circle Time for Mealtime Assistants*, particularly useful, as did the schools I recommended them to as a resource. I also had the opportunity to meet Jenny in 1991 when I attended one of her courses, which was held at the Seely Hotel in Bristol. Attendance on one of Jenny's courses was a joy! Apart from a strengthened belief in the powerful effect of a positive approach it reminded me that fun is an important part of the learning process.

My work on the development of small-group Circle Time sessions for linguistically vulnerable children came about while working in a primary school in Plymouth with Jackie Lowe, senior speech and language therapist. We were both enthused by the idea of putting our joint expertise together to support several children who were linguistically vulnerable through lack of skill development or low confidence in using the skills they did have at their command. We worked closely with their class teacher and by 2001 had planned a series of carefully crafted sessions to develop language, thinking skills and communication. They were widely used in the school using the quality Circle Time ethos (which is entirely positive and seeks to affirm the participants). We then began a similar process in the nursery. By the autumn of 2001 we had a series of courses that I had written up in a way that would be supportive of the adults running it. Evaluations had begun to come in from other schools and nurseries who were trialling the sessions. They indicated pleasing gains made by the children in the groups. These gains had transferred to the classroom/large-group situation.

In looking at the rationale which underlies the principles of the Circle Time as a whole it is important to look at what traditional models of education say about the learning process and to make useful comparisons. I am not the first researcher by any means to arrive at the conclusion that if you use quality Circle Time as the heart of the educational process the resultant learning is many times more effective for the reasons explored below.

The benefits of using Circle Time ethos and practice in small groups to develop thinking and communication skills: an historical perspective

In the 1930s John Dewey promoted the centrality of action and reflection in the learning process. This challenged more traditional models of passive learning where the expectation was upon the student to receive knowledge and later to find ways to apply the knowledge in action (Stevens 2001).

Dewey's emphasis still underpins current thinking by many that the ingredients of effective learning are confidence, activity and reflection, i.e. 'If I believe I can succeed I am willing to get involved in the task. I work at it, I think about it . . . and I realise that as a consequence I have learned a new skill or concept or discovered a new line of enquiry.'

The role of language in education

Paradoxically education has traditionally relied more on teacher talk than on active involvement to transmit knowledge and develop academic and cognitive skills (Goodlad 1984; Sizer 1984). This puts a high demand on learners' ability to use language in order to accommodate information, develop their thinking skills and convey their thinking to others. The last requires a growing level of communication skills.

Some children have particularly low levels of effective language and communication skills at their disposal. They may also have difficulty in adapting their language to meet the demands of formal situations. Much of the instructional language and reflection in the classroom seems to present difficulties for them. The children with these difficulties find themselves unable to frame relevant questions to help their understanding. Their access to even the best curriculum is therefore limited, but where teacher talk is the main medium of transmission the child is effectively excluded from learning, to the frustration of both child and teacher.

Language, friendship and the vulnerable child

Another major area needs to be considered here. It is that low levels of language and communication skills will affect the child's ability to make good relationships with peers and to work collaboratively with them when the need arises.

Not surprisingly, confident, well liked children appear to communicate more effectively than less popular children. A recent study at the University of Texas indicated that popular children were more likely to be those who had good language skills. For example, they tended to communicate clearly by saying the other child's name, establishing eye contact and using appropriate touch to gain attention (Kemple 1992). They replied appropriately to children who spoke to them rather than ignoring the speaker, changing the subject or saying something irrelevant which a less linguistically confident child may well do. They were more likely to accompany refusals with explanations or alternatives, e.g. 'Let's pretend we're hiding from the dragon', 'No, we played that yesterday' or 'No, let's be robbers instead' – rather than just saying no.

Kemple points to an increased likelihood of aggression or conflict due to a lack of verbal reasoning and conflict resolution skills for children who cannot establish a positive place for themselves in the peer culture. All this can detract from the listening classroom and hinders the flow of learning for all.

Overcoming barriers to learning; taking individual learning styles and talents into account

Where language becomes the main method of transmission of academic and social knowledge to the child in education, it is crucial to ensure that the child has the necessary skills and confidence to work with that medium.

Merely introducing activity in group tasks will not be sufficient to ensure that effective learning will take place. There must be consideration of each pupil's differing learning styles and strengths. A learning style is the unique way each person tends to learn most effectively. Some learn best through listening or observing or using visual materials related to the information under study. Some have a greater need to talk through and question. There is also a marked difference in learners along a continuum of activity. Some want to be highly active and hands on, whereas others approach tasks more reflectively.

Learning styles can be harnessed to aid the development of the multiple intelligences or talents which we all have but with varying degrees of skill in each. Broadly seven areas of intelligence have been identified by Howard Gardner, cognitive developmental psychologist and educator. They are:

- linguistic;
- logical–mathematical;
- visual;
- bodily kinaesthetic;
- musical–auditory;
- intrapersonal;
- interpersonal.

Howard Gardner has developed this powerful idea of multiple intelligences as a way to widen thinking about improving school-based learning. There is strong evidence to suggest that the most effective learning takes place when the teaching situation provides opportunities for pupils to develop their areas of strength in these key areas and others and they become excited by learning. The following quote from the Cheshire website makes some important points.

> If we wish to improve learning and human achievement we need to ensure the teaching and learning strategies and experiences are not dominated by instructional models and take account of the whole person, their motivation and their preferred learning modes.

The next task for the pupil is to learn to develop strengths in other areas and use new and different learning strategies. A full description of these intelligences is available in Howard Gardner's book *Frames of Mind*. Articles on the theory of multiple intelligences with self-assessment questionnaires for pupils and teachers are available on the website of Cheshire County Council.

Emotional intelligence and the importance of emotional literacy

Howard Gardner also emphasises the importance of developing our emotional awareness and skills.

People with highly developed emotional intelligence can identify and manage their own emotional responses and have some understanding of the moods, motivation and actions of others. They use their good problem-solving skills to help others and this can result in effective conflict resolution. It is vital to identify a place in the curriculum for such important life skills.

Emotional literacy, to me, means the ability to put words to the many nuances of feeling we experience. It is clear that where pupils do not develop in this area difficulties lie ahead for them. The majority of older pupils I now see for anger management have very few words to describe their emotional states: typically 'chilled out', 'angry' and 'mad'. Bearing in mind that more than 1,500 words related to feelings can be identified, this is a limited and limiting emotional vocabulary and often reflects a lack of awareness of the effects emotion has on the physical being. It limits too the range of responses available to the person.

I work with these students to identify the feelings they have and also the physical signals accompanying them. We then work together to put a wider ranging graded sequence of words to this: for example, chilled out, OK irritated, bothered, disturbed, annoyed, hurt, upset, disbelief, angry, very angry, furious, raging. Once people have in their mind an awareness of a range of emotional descriptors they have more awareness of where a feeling may be leading. They have in addition the words to tell people about how they are feeling. This can ease the emotional pressure. They can then choose more fruitful ways to express their feelings. Angry feelings can become assertive words rather than aggressive action. Thinking has greater clarity when the mind is clear.

There are strong indications that this process of putting words to feelings needs to begin as early as possible, certainly in early primary. A significant thread of our small-group work with young children is the development of both emotional awareness and the language which supports it and allows its expression.

How we put this into practice in the development of our small-group sessions

With the small-group Circle Time we have endeavoured to build sessions which involve the children in ways that allow them to contribute and develop individually according to their preferred learning styles. We have also helped them to develop their least preferred styles so that they begin to be more skilled overall. We value the importance of the positive ethos of Circle Time in providing a safe, relaxed atmosphere. Again to quote Cheshire County Council:

> The brain functions and develops most effectively when meeting challenge in a relaxed, safe environment where recognition, praise and reward outweigh criticism and when it is enabled to process many sensory inputs at once and at many different levels of consciousness.

Our Circle Time groups certainly include movement for a purpose, talking and questioning, music, rhyming, logical critical reasoning and thinking skills, social skills and emotional awareness, and are highly visual. The content involves aspects of all seven areas of intelligence outlined above.

The children initially did not have highly developed listening and concentration skills. But they developed them markedly through the course. For us this signalled that the children had become more motivated and effective learners overall. This was borne out in the classroom later where there was a clear transfer of skills.

Why small-group work?

Many children have benefited from whole-class Circle Time. Having been involved in training I have seen this positive effect. But there are children who seem to freeze in a large group. These vulnerable children often do not appear able to take advantage of the benefits available within the whole-class circle. I had often felt that for some children a preparation for whole-class Circle Time was needed.

Teachers face the challenge of providing effective support for all the children. Whole-class Circle Time has been shown to be effective in helping the majority of pupils but for linguistically vulnerable children barriers need first to be overcome. The main barrier can be a lack of self-belief. Mind and hand may appear to be engaged but the heart may not be if children do not believe that they can do what they are being asked. If children succeed they can see this success as a 'lucky break' or at worst a big pressure because they will be expected to do it again and they are not at all sure that they can repeat it. The child may see in a large group a threat to an already fragile self-esteem and will respond in a self-protective way by trying to disrupt the group activity.

In our work we have found we can harness the Circle Time ethos and activities as part of a small-group process. This gives a strong foundation for improving individual confidence to a level at which the pupil will be able to join in more fully with the class group. We have found that if an appropriately structured small group is available then children can and do acquire necessary skills.

Setting up small-group Circle Time

With the support of the headteacher of a primary school in Plymouth, where I work as an educational psychologist, and with Jackie Lowe, a senior speech and language therapist, and Tracey Palmer, an experienced teacher, a course was built using each of our professional specialisms.

Together we sought to find practical ways of including linguistically vulnerable children from nursery to Key Stage 2 in small-group Circle Time sessions. We felt confident that our programme would address many of the difficulties facing teachers in developing the language, thinking and social skills of identified groups of children.

The programme emphasised above all the traditional supportive Circle Time ethos. It explored and developed each of the areas of language, communication and thinking skills through practical hands on activity and group reflection. Tasks were planned carefully to balance activity and concentration in order to maximise good levels of attention and build listening skills.

What happens in the group

In the small group we were able to be sensitive to the different learning and teaching styles of the children and the staff who became involved in the groups. Each session was crafted to provide a range of learning inputs to meet their needs in every session.

- Each session is based on activities to promote reflection and critical thinking.
- The supportive principles of Circle Time are drawn upon to provide a group ethos in which we can foster the children's confidence in putting ideas forward. The sessions highlight the importance of 'brainstorming'; that is, allowing everyone to bring their ideas to a task before we select (but not judge) the most appropriate answer.
- The levels of activity and focus are carefully balanced to achieve motivation and optimum attention. The pace and language is deliberately slowed down. This has a tremendously positive impact on behaviour as children realise they can access the activities fully.
- The content of the sessions includes phonic work and though not a stand-alone programme it has proved invaluable to the speech therapist who has found children to be more open to working on sounds with her in any individual sessions.
- Language development work, phonics, sound work, thinking skills, prediction, reasoning, hypothesis development and checking effective questioning are integral to the sessions.
- The sessions give opportunities for dynamic assessment of children's needs and progress which can be supplemented in class lessons.
- The relativity of position is looked at, e.g. what is in front of the tree to you may be behind the tree from where I am sitting. We then bring this flexibility of thinking into the area of emotions, e.g. people have a range of emotions and may not feel or respond in the same way as you have responded.
- Listening and turn-taking are an integral part of the course.
- Visualisation and harnessing imagination are introduced as powerful learning tools.
- Speaking with confidence and clarity to an audience and communicating their thinking is an outcome which is carefully planned for.

The course as a whole prepares children for the transition from learning from experience to learning from direct teaching through the medium of discussion by encouraging their ability to listen, to visualise an action or event and to recall and describe events.

What were the effects of the group on the children?

The children became much more skilled and effective thinkers and communicators. The group allowed them to overcome the barriers to learning and allowed them to bring their 'heart, mind and hand' to the task. Learning had been fun and relaxed, and therefore memorable and likely to endure and develop over time.

The children proved highly motivated because of the fun feeling to the group. They found they were concentrating almost without realising and they were contributing ideas. For some this was the first time they had done so well in a group situation.

In the small group we were able to keep the instructional language straightforward and not too demanding. The children blossomed as they found that they could more easily understand the language and slowly the barriers to learning and talking in formal situations went down. The exciting development for us was that the barriers stayed down in everyday class situations. Significant improvements were noted in both their thinking skills and their confidence to communicate their thinking to others. Parents also commented on a difference in the way their children talked. Fuller sentences and well thought out questions were both mentioned.

Teachers often reported that after only four sessions they had noted positive changes in attitude and behaviour. This was borne out by later evaluation of the work. In our experience teachers have expressed pleasant surprise that children with such obvious linguistic vulnerability should progress so markedly in such a short time.

What support is needed after the group?

For the child who will no longer be supported through the small group, two things should be considered as paramount. It is important to draw the experience to a definite close and make farewells with concrete reminders for each member of the group. It is also supportive to ensure that the child returns to quality Circle Time in the classroom with a similarly supportive affirming ethos. Jenny Mosley's training courses contain a highly effective five-step model for whole-class Circle Time.

From a speech and language therapist's viewpoint

These 25-30 minutes of quality interaction time on a regular basis provide an invaluable and rewarding method of tying many aspects of language development together within a busy school setting.

The children chosen for these groups were those most vulnerable in terms of listening and language skills. The fact that each session can be repeated a second or third time allows for a spiral learning effect and enables the children involved to grasp and then feel confident with the issues being addressed.

All the children enjoyed this approach. They gained valuable insights into interaction as part of communication, emphasising how each individual has equal value and how important eye contact, turn-taking, listening skills and individual thinking are to communication. They also have the opportunity to build and expand on additional areas of expressive language skills, including:

- phonological awareness;
- the value of questioning skills;
- exploring language use associated with emotion and empathy;
- the development of visualisation in basic story-telling.

All the children involved gained in self-esteem and in the ability to think and question for themselves, as well as becoming more linguistically fluid and expressive.

This is a good, enjoyable practice that can have a remarkable impact on many children.

Jackie Lowe, Speech and Language Therapist

Policy: putting circle groups into your school

School policy needs to reflect children's needs and how the school intends to address them. By using the structured groupwork sessions we have developed, we find that these needs are wonderfully met.

As the small-group Circle Time has been so successful in many school settings, I would definitely recommend that Circle Time in small groups structured in this way becomes part of the school policy and practice. The following discussions have taken place, which will vary from school to school.

Should small-group Circle Time go into the PSHE policy? Yes, of course. We need to give the opportunity to all children to develop their social and thinking skills to promote positive thoughts, actions and feelings. Some linguistically vulnerable children do need the ethos and pace of the small support group sessions to enable them to access the wider curriculum, including PSHE.

Should small-group Circle Time be entered into the positive behaviour policy? Yes, of course. It provides an excellent opportunity to address attitudinal change upon which behavioural change depends and which is often the most difficult to achieve.

Should small-group Circle Time be entered into the literacy and numeracy strategy? Yes, of course. Every element for the speaking and listening attainment target is being fulfilled with the structured course which has been developed, with children having time and confidence to express themselves orally without fear of failure. This type of Circle Time also addresses, to some extent, basic vocabulary, supports children with a range of speech difficulties and includes basic numerical activities and language.

Should small-group Circle Time be included in the 'citizenship' policy? Yes, of course. Working together as a group over a long period brings children together and gives them a sense of belonging upon which can be built bridges to the class, school, home and wider community.

Therefore small-group Circle Time for this purpose is an entirety in itself. It should not be thought of as placed solely in one policy as it also fits so well with other curriculum areas. But school policy is there to ensure that the children's needs are enumerated and structured and positive ways forward recommended. Within this it is our role to ensure that all children have the best possible chance of achieving their true potential by putting appropriate resources and activities in place. This is especially true where teachers need to develop children's basic understanding in a system where language is the main means of transmission and where the main difficulty the children have is poor comprehension and expression of the spoken word.

Tracey Palmer, Teacher

How to use this book

Who are the intended group?

- The course contained in this book was developed to aid linguistically challenged children, the children who find it difficult to understand verbal instructions and who do not have the skills or confidence to frame questions to clarify their understanding, or to speak out in a large group.
- The activities in the sessions are set to achieve a balance of movement and focus, to maintain concentration and repetition and to help achieve mastery – a range of concepts, skills and processes are developed through the games.
- Over and above this, the children develop confidence in themselves as learners – this confidence carries over to other situations including the classroom.

Before running the groups

1 Involve staff in discussion about the aims of the group and children who would benefit from inclusion in the group.
2 Involve parents and carers. Seek parental permission if an outside agency is involved in running the group with the school.
3 Assess: (a) take a snapshot of the children's strengths and difficulties with the individual assessment form provided on page xxiii, using one copy for each pupil. (b) plan targets through group IEPs. Individual IEPs can be used where appropriate.
4 Identify two people who will be running the group. This is a necessity, not a luxury.
5 Create a box of resources to keep on hand for the group. Photocopiable materials contained in the Appendix will need to be enlarged to A3. This is important.

When running the group

6 Record attendance at sessions on page xxii.
7 When the first session starts tell the children how special their group is. This is an opportunity to give lots of positive messages.
8 Follow the golden keys, Pause, Ponder, Use Praise Phrases, slow the Pace.
9 At the end of each half-term reassess the children on the scales you have chosen and review the group IEPs.

10 For the last group session include a farewell followed up with drawings of things the children have especially enjoyed so that they have a concrete reminder for as long as they need it.

Using the materials: flexibility

When using the materials go by the level that you feel your group of children are at. There will be some groups of children who need repetition of sessions and some groups who need to start sessions at a higher level.

Broadly speaking the sessions in the book are divided into three sections but needs can vary. All groups of children can vary in their needs and you may find that in one nursery the children work happily at the nursery-level sessions whereas in another they have mastered the basic concepts therein and need to work on the concepts contained in the Key Stage 1 sessions.

In our experience some sessions will sometimes need to be repeated three or more times, whereas another session at the same level is assimilated in the first presentation.

Bibliography

Barnes, D. and Todd, G. (1977) *Language and Communication in Small Groups*. London: Routledge and Kegan Paul.

Cheshire County Council Website. http://www.salt.cheshire.org.uk

Gardner, H. (1993a) *Frames of Mind: The Theory of Multiple Intelligences*. Canada: HarperCollins Canada Limited.

Gardner, H. (1993b) *Multiple Intelligences: The Theory in Practice*. Canada: HarperCollins Canada Limited.

Goodlad (1984) Sizer (1984) *Changing Schools' Expertise in Education*. Eric Digests ED345929 (Internet).

Kann Yeok-Hwa, N. (1998) *Enhancing Student Thinking Through Collaborative Learning*. Eric Digests ED422586 (Internet).

Kemple, K. (1992) *Understanding and Facilitating Pre-school Children's Peer Acceptance*. Eric Digests ED345866 (Internet).

Mosley, J. (1993) *Turn Your School Round*. Cambridge: LDA.

Mosley, J. (1996) *Quality Circle Time in the Primary School*. Cambridge: LDA.

Stevens, Walker-Richards (2001) Eric Digests, 14 May. ED345929.

Western Australian Education Department. For the basic idea for Toni's Balloons.

Resources

Talkabout series; Talkabout the Playground; Pragmatics; Feelings

Available from Black Sheep Press
67 Middleton, Cowling, Keighley, West Yorks BD22 0DQ
Tel: 01535 631346
e mail: alan@blacksheeppress.co.uk
www.blacksheep-epress.com

Spirals language development group attendance record

Date of session	Session no.	Run by	Children who attended

Name .... **Class** ....

Please could you write a brief description about the child's present level of attainment in each of the following skills. You will be asked to repeat this activity in six weeks, therefore it would be helpful if, during the time, you could note any significant developments in any of the following areas and note them down next time.

Thank you.

Skill	Present level (1)	Present level (2)
Thinking skills Child's ability to plan own actions		
Language skills How and what language is used		
Social skills Attitude and response towards peers		
Listening skills Ability to listen and concentrate in class/group situations		
Classroom Confidence, responses and general performance in the classroom		

List of materials which will need preparation before a session

Materials which will need some preparation prior to the session (all the other materials are usually readily available in Nurseries and classrooms).

NURSERY

Sessions 1 – end
Several brightly coloured cloths, e.g. plastic tablecloths/fabric/printed fabric (possibly printed by the children)/net curtaining etc.

Session 5
Big and little animals, identical in all but size

Session 7
- Feely bag – things we eat/things we do not eat,
  e.g. apple, bread, sweet potato/rock, fir cone, shell, cup. Picture of someone eating
- Jingle band made of elastic and small bells

Session 8
- Feely bag – round shapes/square shapes (round and square shapes all same colour)

Session 10 – Cut out long/short arm/legs/hair

Session 11
- 2 pieces of ribbon or tinsel, long/short
- Enlarge Twinkle Star picture in Appendix to A3

Session 12
- Feely bag – things we wear/do not wear
- Picture of a person
- Tube for Incy Spider

KS1

Session 3
- Houses can be square blocks with triangles for roof
Feely bag – objects or pictures of the at family of words, e.g. cat, bat
Some of these are obtainable from the ELS folder resource pictures

Session 6 – Feely bag – pictures or objects of the [in] family of words, e.g. tin, pin

Sessions 7 and 11 – Feely bag – objects with initial sounds 's' and 'p'
- 4 pictures of Annie (shocked, angry, happy, sad) photocopied from Appendix

Session 8
- Copies of story picture of Annie on the beach with her dog, photocopied from Appendix (enough for one between two children)
- Photocopy of Toni holding her balloons enlarged to A3. Balloons should previously have been colour coded to match with question circles, as explained in the text
- Question circles colour coded to large picture and cut out into individual circles
- Stand up box to pin it to

Session 9
- Pictures from the Pragmatics pack can be ordered from Black Sheep Press (address in Resources, page xxi)

Sessions 10/11
One set of Mr Bears Question Cards, photocopied from Appendix enlarged to A3
They can made more user friendy by putting symbols onto them to aid recognition by children

KS 2

Session 13
- Photocopies of Storyline pictures of spider, teddy, bed, tree, etc. from the Appendix
- Cards depicting objects of the [at] and [house] family of words

Session 15
Photocopies of Storyline pictures again, objects beginning with 'ch' and 'f'.

Session 16
Prepare cards showing mouse/hedgehog/butterfly. These can be taken from page 77 and enlarged if wished
- Photocopy dragon from Appendix if wished, enlarged to A3

Session 17
- Feely bag – object cards of the [at] family of words
- Playground picture from Talkabout Playgrounds, available to order from Black Sheep Press

Session 18
- Playground pictures again
- Toni's Balloons – photocopy picture from Appendix of Toni holding her balloons, enlarged to A3. Balloons should previously have been colour coded to match with question circles, as explained in the text
- 4 syllable cards again

Session 19
- Mr Bear's Question Cards from Appendix, enlarged to A3 and cut out
- Pragmatics Pictures (as used in Session KSI/9), available to order from Black Sheep Press
- Picture of dragon photocopied from Appendix

Session 20
- Talkabout Playgrounds as in Sessions 17 and 18
- Rhyme cards at and an words

Session 21
- Storyline pictures photocopied from Appendix
- Cards with pictures of objects in the at and house family of words

Session 22
- Drawing of a happy person
- Talkabout Playgrounds Question Sheet 2: a little boy showing his picture to his class
- Syllable cards, mouse, hedgehog, butterfly, dog, weasel

Session 23
- Objects with initial sound ch and sh
- Pictures of Annie photocopied from Appendix

Session 24
- Picture of a worried child (from the Black Sheep Pragmatics Pack)
- Mr Bear's Question Cards from Appendix photocopied and cut out

Sessions for Nursery

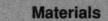

Materials

Are listed at the start of each session and are readily available in nurseries.

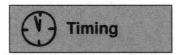

Timing

Twenty to 30 minutes depending on the length of time spent on each game.

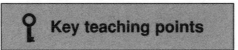

Key teaching points

It is essential to keep the pace of your language slow. Use 'pondering' to gain attention and interest and to slow down the pace. Also essential is keeping language as uncluttered and simple as possible. An example of this would be instead of saying

Adam has chosen the elephant. Tell us why you like the elephant best, Adam

simplify it to

Adam likes the elephant because...

There is a clear role for us in extending children's language but in the language group we are getting down to the basics of language and ensuring that the children have a good grasp at that level. To do so we need to keep our language at that level in the group to give the children access to the concepts we are teaching.

The language will become more complex as the children gain confidence and skills.

Language concepts

The aim of these nursery sessions is to feed the children's knowledge bank and support the development of structures to enable critical thinking and reasoning. At this stage we are concentrating on feeding their knowledge and

1

gradually encouraging them to express what they know. It will be clear from their responses to activities whether they have grasped the concepts involved or not. This is a useful form of assessment. Concepts can then be worked on in the week and reassessed in the following group sessions.

Visual cues

Children have different learning strengths. Some learn best from hearing information, some from having it presented visually and some from activity-based tasks. Pre-school children learn best when all three aspects are present and learning is substantially supported by visual materials and activities and rhythm. For this reason the nursery sessions are designed to be active and visual with familiar rhymes. You can help the process greatly by using simple gesture to accompany descriptions and instructions.

Praise

Praise every child at least twice in each session.

Praise for good sitting before the group becomes too fidgety. Offer to sprinkle imaginary 'magic glue dust' for a child who has difficulty in sitting still.

Positive

Try not to say, 'No, that's wrong.' Clearly there are right and wrong answers, but the group works on similar principles to brainstorming where all ideas are listened to and considered, and then an answer is chosen from all the ideas. We tend to say, 'Thank you, you spoke up really well. You gave me another idea.'

Giving time to think

When you expect a child to answer a question give him or her at least 15 seconds to respond. (You will be surprised how long that seems!) Encourage with comments such as:

You are thinking really well. Well done!

You are quiet and you are thinking about this really well!

If the child doesn't answer, offer support by asking:

Would you like some help from us?

If yes, ask the group (adults included) to put up their hands if they want to help give an answer. The child then chooses someone.

Fun

Enjoy this time with the children.

Behaviour

Try, when changing the activity and the pace of the activity, to change the focus and distract from negative behaviour if it occurs. Praise the other children for behaviour that you do want to see. Try not to introduce a competitive element.

Main concepts covered in Nursery sessions

Session 1   Memorisation. Coordination of physical action with speaking.
Understanding and use of **under** and **up**.
Taking care of each other (social skills).
Using language. Extending utterances.

Session 2   Memorisation. Coordination of physical action with speaking.
Listening to, and acting on, instructions.
Understanding and use of **under** and **up**.
Awareness of words sounding the same at the end (beginning of rhyming awareness).
Emotional awareness.

Session 3   Memorisation. Coordination of physical action with speaking.
Using language. Extending utterances.
Understanding of the concept **over**, using the word over, assessing use of the words over/under.
Emotional awareness.

Session 4   Memorisation. Coordination of physical action with speaking.
Listening to, and acting on, instructions.
Understanding and use of **on** and **under**.
Using language. Extending utterances.
Saying 'goodbye'.

Session 5   Memorisation. Coordination of physical action with speaking.
Understanding and use of **big** and **little**.
Using language. Extending utterances.
Understanding and use of **full**.

Session 6   Memorisation. Coordination of physical action with speaking.
Understanding and use of **under**.
Extending to sentences. Turn-taking, energising and confidence.
Extending speaking and encourage expressive language.
Develop the **why/because** link.
Sound production '*p*'.
Understanding of **heavy** and **full** and their properties.

Session 7	Memorisation. Coordination of physical action with speaking.
	Categorisation (things we eat).
	Understanding and use of **up** and **down**.
	Sound production 'k'.
	Relate **empty** and **full**.

Session 8	Memorisation. Coordination of physical action with speaking.
	Understanding and use of **under**.
	Categorisation (**round** and **square**).
	Awareness of rhyme.
	Body parts.
	Cooperative task. Positive emotion.

Session 9	Memorisation. Coordination of physical action with speaking.
	Understanding and use of **on** and **under**.
	Using language. Extending utterances.
	Extending to sentences. Turn-taking, energising and confidence.
	Sequencing. Colour names **red** and **blue**.

Session 10	Memorisation. Coordination of physical action with speaking.
	Extending to sentences. Turn-taking, energising and confidence.
	Understanding and use of **long** and **short**.
	Emotional awareness.

Session 11	Memorisation. Coordination of physical action with speaking.
	Understanding and use of **long** and **short**.
	Sound production 'k'.
	Use of questions.
	Extending to sentences. Turn-taking, energising and confidence.
	Awareness and use of **heavy**.

Session 12	Memorisation. Coordination of physical action with speaking.
	Categorisation (things we wear).
	Understanding and use of **inside** and **outside**.
	Using language. Extending utterances.
	Understanding and use of **top** and **bottom**.
	Sequencing. Colour names **red** and **blue**.

Nursery Session 1

MATERIALS NEEDED

- Ball.
- A large, brightly coloured cloth (big enough for the group to sit under). If there are two adults in the group you will need one to lead the children round, so tuck one end of the cloth under books on top of a cupboard and hold the other end to make a bridge.
- Bear.

Please keep language pace *slow* and *simple*. Use 'pondering' to slow your pace and invite shared thought. Praise throughout the session. Say a little about how well children came in and joined you.

Opening round: name game

(Getting to know the group, sitting down)

Tell the children you need to know their names so you will play a name game. Roll a ball across the circle a few times. Say your name and roll it to a child. Encourage the child to say his or her name and roll the ball to someone else and so on for several minutes until all have had a chance to roll the ball. The aim is to be able to say: 'My name is . . .'

Recap on all the names. Introduce the idea of the group working together for several sessions. Stand in the circle.

Nursery rhyme

(To encourage awareness of rhyming)
(Sitting)

> **use praise phrases**

Hold hands in a circle. Walk round in a circle singing the rhyme together:

> Twinkle, twinkle little Star,
> How I wonder what you are
> Up above the world so high
> Like a diamond in the sky
> Twinkle, twinkle little Star
> How I wonder what you are.

Ponder that some of the words sound the same: high, sky; Star, are.

Sing the rhyme again. Leave out the last word 'are', letting the children sing it. Comment that they remembered/sang the word 'are', the word that sounds like 'Star'. (At this point you are first raising awareness of the way words can rhyme.)

Under

Sit with the children and show them how to make a rainstorm by patting their knees (see **Pitter patter** below). Tell them you are going to make a tent by holding the cloth over their heads (two adults hold the cloth over the children). Ask what the children can see when they are *under* the cloth when they look up. Tell a simple story (waving the cloth) about the wind blowing and the rain falling. Encourage the children to 'Pitter patter'. Then the rain gets softer. The wind goes away and (lift the cloth away) the sun comes out.

Pitter patter

Show the children how to make the sound of rain by patting their hands on their knees. Pat harder as you talk about the rain falling harder, then diminish as the rain stops. Finish by gently rubbing the palms of your hands together to make a 'ssh' sound.

Trains

(Children sit in a circle. Adults stand)

Explain that you are going to be the engine of the train. Go to each child and ask 'Will you join my train?' The child is encouraged to say 'Yes' or 'Yes I will' and they join on behind you. If a child refuses twice use your knowledge of that child to decide whether to pass on again or encourage to join in. When everyone is on the train – chug round – then come to rest in a circle again.

Closing round

(Standing)

Bear hugs: pass a bear round to give him a hug to make him happy.

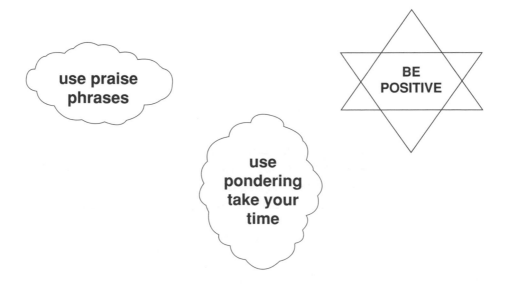

use praise phrases

use pondering take your time

BE POSITIVE

Nursery Session 2

MATERIALS NEEDED
- Ball.
- Sheet of paper, a pen and Blu-tack for Golden reminders.
- Piece of fruit, preferably real, for each child (you may need a few spare pieces in case some get squashed).
- Large brightly coloured cloth (big enough for the group to sit under together).
- Bear.

Please keep language pace *slow* and *simple*. Use 'pondering' to slow your pace and invite shared thought. Praise throughout the session. Praise good sitting, and if some children become restless, praise *good* sitting even more.

Roll the ball

(Sitting down)

Say your name and roll the ball to someone else in the group, e.g. 'My name is Jack.' (If the children are skilled in this they can say their name and who they will roll it to: 'My name is Tom and I will roll it to Angela.') Encourage children to say the sentence, but don't insist.

Praise good sitting.

Fruit basket game

(Standing up)

Play once or twice to energise and focus the group.

Stand up in a circle. An adult walks around the circle and gives each child a fruit and names it (keep to two for simplicity). Thus: apple, orange, apple, orange. Include adults in this. Check that children remember what fruit they have:

Hands up apples. Hands up oranges. Sit down apples, hands on heads etc.

Then:

In a minute we are going to change places. I will say apples change and all apples move to a new place in the circle. Then oranges will have a turn. Now, apples change.

Focus children on what you want by commenting on positive behaviour. Comment on children walking quietly and carefully across the circle. Show by example where necessary.

Oranges change.

Comment on positive behaviour in walking sensibly, taking care of other people in the circle, making space for someone, thinking about what they are doing. When playing this game in later sessions extend the language, e.g. 'Apples, find a new place.'

Golden reminders

(Two minutes only)

Remind the group how pleased you are with their careful feet, thinking ears, watching eyes and thinking brain.

> To draw out from the group, ask
> 'What do you do with your eyes?' Draw out 'looking'.
> 'What do you do with your ears?' Draw out 'listening'.
> 'What do you do with your feet?' Draw out 'walking'.
> You were looking carefully and walking carefully to look after each other.

Write on the paper: listening ears, looking eyes, careful feet (with a simple drawing beside each).

Nursery rhyme

(To encourage awareness of rhyming)
(Sitting)

use praise phrases

Hold hands in a circle. Walk round in a circle singing the rhyme together:

> Twinkle, twinkle little Star,
> How I wonder what you are
> Up above the world so high
> Like a diamond in the sky
> Twinkle, twinkle little Star
> How I wonder what you are.

Ponder that some of the words sound the same: high, sky; Star, are.
    Sing the rhyme again. Leave out the last word 'are', letting the children sing it. Comment that they remembered/sang the word 'are', the word that sounds like 'Star'. (At this point you are first raising awareness of the way words can rhyme.)

Under the cloth

(Checking understanding and encouraging expression)

(Moving round)

Using a large cloth, two people hold the cloth like a bridge. Sing

We go <u>under</u> the cloth
<u>under</u> the cloth
<u>under</u> the cloth.
We go <u>under</u> the cloth
<u>under</u> we go.

(To the tune of 'Here we go round the mulberry bush')

As you sing, one person leads the children underneath the cloth behind each other in a line holding hands. Join hands to form a ring and walk under the cloth. To begin with you will need an adult leading the children in a ring, walking round and going under the cloth. So to make a bridge with the cloth, you can secure one end of the cloth on top of a cupboard and hold the other end. This leaves the other adult free to lead the children round. The cloth is being held so that it just brushes their heads as they go underneath it. Sing twice. At the end of each verse look under the cloth, saying 'Who is under the cloth now?' Ask 'What can you see when you look up?'

All under

(To broaden conceptual understanding and expression)

Tell the children we can all go under the cloth together. Two people hold the edges while the group gather in the middle to sit under the cloth. Say 'Where are you all? Oh, you're all under, under the cloth. Can you say that word? Yes that's right – under. You're all under.' (This gives the opportunity for them to experience and then to put a word to the concept.)

Praise good sitting.

Create an atmosphere by describing the wind blowing and moving the cloth up and down. Then the rain starts (tap your lap to simulate the sound of the rain and encourage the children to join in).

Gather back in the circle again.

(Optional) Invite interested children to sit under the cloth in ones or twos. Ask child 'What can you see when you look up?'

Closing round

Bear hugs. Introduce a bear who wants hugs. (You can ask the children for a range of ideas on what cheers them up if they are sad.) Pass him round the circle to each child. Say how happy he is now they have hugged him.

Nursery Session 3

MATERIALS NEEDED

- Ball.
- Large brightly coloured cloth.
- Gerald Giraffe and two small obstacles, e.g. table, tree.
- Bear.

Please keep language pace *slow* and *simple*. Use 'pondering' to slow your pace and invite shared thought. Praise throughout the session.

Opening round

(Getting to know the group; sitting down)

Say your name and roll the ball to someone else in the group, e.g. 'My name is Jack.' (If the children are skilled in this they can say their name and who they will roll it to: 'My name is Tom and I will roll it to Angela.') Encourage children to say the sentence but don't insist.

Nursery rhyme

(To develop awareness of rhyme)

Walk round in a circle holding hands singing:

> Incy Wincy spider
> climbing up the spout,
> down came the rain
> and washed the spider out.
> Out came the sun
> and dried up all the rain,
> Incy Wincy spider
> Climbs up the spout again.

Ponder that some of the words sound the same: spout, out; rain, again.

Sing the rhyme again. Leave out the last word 'again', letting the children sing it. Comment that they remembered/sang the word 'again', the word that sounds like 'rain'. (At this point you are first raising awareness of the way words can rhyme.)

use pondering take your time

Over

(Moving around)

Place the cloth on the floor in the middle of the circle. Explain 'We will go *over* the cloth today.'

Organise children, so that they follow you. Sing (to the tune of 'Here we go round the mulberry bush').

> We are walking <u>over</u> the cloth
> <u>over</u> the cloth, <u>over</u> the cloth.
> We are walking <u>over</u> the cloth
> <u>over</u> the cloth we go.

Stand in the circle. Ask how else we could move. Pause, encourage ideas from the group, then give ideas if needed, e.g. hop, skip, jump.

EITHER 1. Choose one way of moving, then as before organise the children to follow you, e.g.

> We are skipping <u>over</u> the cloth
> <u>over</u> the cloth, <u>over</u> the cloth.
> We are skipping <u>over</u> the cloth
> <u>over</u> the cloth we go.

OR 2. Invite individual children to jump, hop, etc. over the cloth. Sit in the circle.

> We went <u>over</u> the cloth. Can you say <u>over</u>? Yes that's right, <u>over</u>, we went <u>over</u> the cloth.

Jumping animals

Introduce an animal. Place two obstacles, e.g. box and tree, in the middle of the circle. Tell the following story with actions.

> This is Gerald Giraffe. He ran through the woods. It was easy. Then he saw a big box on the ground. He could not run through it, so he jumped over it. Then he ran and ran till he saw a fence. He could not run through it so he jumped over it.

Praise good sitting.

Invite children to help Gerald to jump over the box. For example, 'Anita, can you help Gerald jump over the box?' 'Bob, can you help Gerald jump over the fence?' End by saying how happy Gerald is now that they have helped him.

use praise phrases

11

Choose over and under

(Functional use of the concept word)

Children form a circle line. Two people hold the cloth like a bridge. Each child chooses whether to go over or under the cloth as they go past. Before the child gets to the adult he or she has to call out **'over' or 'under'**. The adult responds by raising or lowering the cloth to allow the child to go over or under.

Make sure each child has a turn.

Closing round

Bear hugs. Introduce a bear who wants hugs. Pass him round the circle to each child. Say how happy he is now they have hugged him.

Preparing to go back to the large group:

Ask each child to tell you what they will play with when they go back. You can use photographs of activities to prompt them.

BE
POSITIVE

Nursery Session 4

MATERIALS NEEDED

- Ball.
- Piece of imitation fruit for each person in the group.
- Cuddly animal.
- Tea towel size cloth.

Please keep language pace *slow* and *simple*. Use 'pondering' to slow your pace and invite shared thought. Praise throughout the session.

Roll the ball

Say your name and roll the ball to someone else in the group, e.g. 'My name is Jack.' (If the children are skilled in this they can say their name and who they will roll it to: 'My name is Tom and I will roll it to Angela.') Encourage children to say the sentence. Praise good sitting.

use praise phrases

Nursery rhyme

(To develop awareness of rhyming)

(Standing)

> I'm a little teapot
> short and stout.
> Here's my handle
> and here's my spout.
> Now the water's boiling
> hear me shout
> 'Tip me up
> and pour me out.'

Ponder that some of the words sound almost the same. Repeat the words: **stout, spout, out**. Ponder that they don't mean the same thing but sound almost the same when we say them.

use pondering take your time

On and under the small cloth

(Widening the concept from own experience)

Pass round a bag of objects. Each child pulls one out and holds it. Put a small cloth in the middle of the circle. Invite children to put their object <u>on</u> the cloth.

Ponder about the fact that they are all <u>on</u> the cloth. 'Can you say the word <u>on</u>?'

Tell the children 'We will put them all back in the bag.' Pass the bag round so that they can put their object back.

Pass the bag round again. This time ask each child to choose where they will put their object: 'under or on?' When the child has made their choice encourage them to say whether their object is on or under. A one-word response is acceptable at this stage. Encourage children to **use** the language. Praise good sitting.

Fruit basket: apple, orange, banana

Have a piece of fruit for each child. Walk round the circle and give one to each child individually. Say the name of the fruit and invite the child, by your tone of voice and smile, to repeat it back to you (but don't insist at this stage). To check that the children know their fruit name, play as follows.

Give the instructions: 'Sit down apples.' Help the children to get this right, then move on to 'Sit down oranges', then 'Sit down bananas.' Then move on to: stand up apples, stand up bananas, turn round apples etc.

Play a few times until you feel the majority of children are confident with the name of their fruit.

> In a minute we are going to change places. I will say, apples change and all apples move to a new place in the circle. Then oranges will have a turn, then bananas. Now, apples change.

Focus children on what you want by commenting on positive behaviour. Comment on children walking quietly and carefully across the circle.

Closing round

(Sitting down)

Pass the cuddly animal round to say 'Goodbye' to.

Prepare to go back to the Nursery by asking children what they want to play with when they go back.

BE
POSITIVE

14

Nursery Session 5

Please keep language pace *slow* and *simple*. Use 'pondering' to slow your pace and invite shared thought. Praise throughout the session.

Roll the ball

Say your name and roll the ball to someone else in the group, e.g. 'My name is Jack.' (If the children are skilled in this they can say their name and who they will roll it to: 'My name is Tom and I will roll it to Angela.') Encourage children to say the sentence. Praise good sitting.

use praise phrases

Big and little

Place two objects that are identical in all but size (animals are the best choice, or any other objects which are identical) in the middle of the circle, and reinforce the words **big** and **little**. 'This is a big lion and a little lion!' Ask the children in turn to touch the big animal (or object) or the little animal. 'Paul, which one is big?' 'Alishia, which one is little?'

The big cat and the little mouse

(Widening the concepts big *and* little*)*

With actions, tell the story of a cat who lived with a mouse. The mouse said to the cat, 'I want to be big like you. Can you teach me how?' The cat said, 'Stretch up like this on tip toe and blow out your cheeks [model this and spread your arms and legs wide] and you will be big like me.' Invite the children to do the same.

Emphasise and repeat the word 'big'. Now reverse the process – talk about the mouse wanting to be little again. Model this. Invite the children to join in making themselves as small as they can curl up. Repeat this several times.

Big and little

Using a large and a small animal, help the children to identify them by size and then show them to you. 'Can you show me the little one?' 'Can you show me the big one?'

Nursery rhyme

(Awareness of rhyme)

(Sitting)

Sing the rhyme together with gestures:

> Twinkle, twinkle little Star,
> How I wonder what you are.
> Up above the world so high
> Like a diamond in the sky.
> Twinkle, twinkle little Star
> How I wonder what you are.

Ponder that some of the words sound the same: high, sky; Star, are. Repeat the rhyme again. Leave out the rhyming words letting the children sing them. Comment that they remembered/sang the words 'sky' and 'are'. At this point you are first raising awareness of the way words can rhyme.

use
pondering
take your
time

Closing round

Pass a small full plate of beads. If the plate is quite full the children will need to pass the plate carefully. Talk about 'full' as the plate goes round.

BE
POSITIVE

Nursery Session 6

Please keep language pace *slow* and *simple*. Use 'pondering' to slow your pace and invite shared thought. Praise throughout the session.

Roll the ball

Say your name and roll the ball to someone else in the group, e.g. 'My name is Jack.' (If the children are skilled in this they can say their name and who they will roll it to: 'My name is Tom and I will roll it to Angela.') Encourage children to say the sentence. Praise good sitting.

use praise phrases

Under

(Checking and developing understanding of concept)

(Moving round)

Using a large cloth, two people hold the cloth like a bridge. Sing (to the tune of 'Here we go round the mulberry bush'):

> We go <u>under</u> the cloth
> <u>under</u> the cloth
> <u>under</u> the cloth.
> We go <u>under</u> the cloth
> <u>under</u> we go.

As you sing, one person leads the children underneath the cloth behind each other in a line holding hands. Join hands to form a ring and walk round the adult and under the cloth. The cloth is held so that it just brushes their heads as they go underneath it. Sing twice. At the end of each verse look under the cloth saying 'Who is under the cloth now?' Ask 'What can you see when you look up?'

Tiger under

*(Using the words **under** and **on** in a relaxed situation – the tiger takes the blame for mistakes!)*

Introduce a tiger with an obstacle (e.g. table, box) that he can go under or on top of. Put some pretend 'food' under the obstacle. Choose a child to guide the tiger to his food. 'Can you help the tiger find his food?' Tiger asks the children 'Is my food on the table or under the table?' Choose a child to look, see the food (e.g. on the table) and say to the tiger where he needs to look, e.g. 'It's on the table.'

The tiger makes a mistake (to encourage participation), then is guided by the children to the right place.

Repeat several times.

Trains

(Turn-taking, energising, confidence)

(Children sit in circle. Adults stand)

Explain that you are going to be the engine of the train. Go to each child and ask 'Will you join my train?' The child is encouraged to say 'Yes' or 'Yes I will' and they join on behind you. If a child refuses twice use your knowledge of that child to decide whether to pass on again or encourage to join in. When everyone is on the train, chug round then come to rest in a circle again.

I like this animal

(To extend speaking and encourage expressive language and develop the 'because' link.)

(Sitting down)

Put two animals in the middle of the circle. Take your time to consider which you like best and why: 'I like the bear because he is furry.' Then, 'Ahmed, which do you like?' When the child points or picks up one animal say 'Ahmed likes the lion because...?' Then blend in the child's response. 'Ahmed likes the lion because it has a tail.'

Fun with sounds

(Encourage confidence in early sound production.)

(Standing up)

Use '*p*' (soft sound as you say '*p*'; avoid using the letter sound or 'puh'). 'Put' a '*p*' sound on to your forefinger. Pass it to the next person and put it on to their forefinger saying '*p*'. Pass round the circle.

BE
POSITIVE

18

Closing round

(Comparing 'full'/'empty' and some properties)

(Sitting down)

Pass an empty dish or plate. Say how easy it is to pass. If there is time, pass a full plate of beads. Talk about it being heavy as well as the need to be more careful when passing it.

use pondering take your time

MATERIALS NEEDED

- Ball.
- Feely bag containing things we eat (e.g. apple, bread, sweet) and also things not in that category (e.g. stone, fir cone, cup).
- Neutral colour hoop or circle of wool or string.
- Picture of someone eating.
- Small object for each child to place in a dish for the closing round.
- Large bunch of keys.
- You will need a 'jingle band'. Obtain a 4-metre piece of thin elastic (decorate simply with a felt tip pen if you wish). Attach 15 small bells and tie it to form a circle. (These materials can usually be tracked down in sewing shops or markets – the cost is under £2.)

Closed bells

Please keep language pace *slow* and *simple*. Use 'pondering' to slow your pace and invite shared thought. Praise throughout the session.

Roll the ball

(Focusing in)

Say your name and roll the ball to someone else in the group, e.g. 'My name is Jack.' (If the children are skilled in this they can say their name and who they will roll it to: 'My name is Tom and I will roll it to Angela.') Encourage children to say the sentence. Praise good sitting.

use praise phrases

Things we eat

(Categorisation)

A feely bag containing things we eat with two objects not in that category is used. There should be one object for each person in the group. In the middle of the circle lay a hoop (or circle of wool or string) and a shallow box lid. Place a picture of someone eating in the hoop.

The feely bag is passed around. The first child takes an object out of the bag. The group decides if it is something we eat. If so it is placed in the hoop. If not it is put in the box lid.

Up and down jingles

(Tactile and fun – encourages awareness of concepts 'up'/'down')

(Standing up)

Using a length of thin elastic with small bells attached, play as follows. All hold the jingles ring. Shake it. Then, to the tune of 'London Bridge is falling down', sing

> Hold the jingles way up high
> Way up high
> Way up high
> Hold the jingles way up high
> Up up up.
>
> Hold the jingles way down low
> Way down low
> Way down low
> Hold the jingles way down low
> Down down down.

Mummy's keys

(Sound of 'k' to help to develop this sound, which can be difficult for some children to make in the back of the mouth)

Show the children a bunch of keys. Tell the story as follows:

Mummy went to the shops to buy some food.
    She came home with a heavy bag of food.
    'Oh good,' she thought, 'I am very tired but I will soon be home and have a nice cup of tea. That will make me happy.'
    She tried to unlock the door with her keys. But when she tried to open the door with her keys, it went 'k'. [Be careful to make the noise in the back of your mouth. Remember not to say the letter name.]
    Mummy said, 'Oh dear, I don't know which one is the right key. I will have to try them all,' and she was a bit worried.
    Can you help mummy to try the keys and make her happy?

Put the bunch of keys in the middle of the circle. Ask a child to pretend to be Mum using the wrong key. Encourage them to make the sound 'k' as you did. Then, each time, ask the group to make the sound together, then ask another child to pretend to try a key. The child can then choose the next child to try the key.
    When you are satisfied that everyone has been involved, find the right key and open the door and let Mum have her cup of tea! Talk lightly about Mum being pleased, relieved, happy when she found the right key.

Closing round

(Adding as a concept and changing the properties by adding)

Each child has a small object (brick, bead etc.). Say the plate is empty, as a plate is passed along each child puts his or her object in the plate and passes it to the next person. Ponder on the fact that the plate is <u>not empty</u> now, it is <u>full</u>.

use
pondering
take your
time

BE
POSITIVE

Nursery Session 8

MATERIALS NEEDED

- Large brightly coloured cloth and small cloth.
- Toy animal.
- Feely bag containing *same colour* round and square shapes.
- Large holed threading beads or bricks – one for each child.

Please keep language pace *slow* and *simple*. Use 'pondering' to slow your pace and invite shared thought. Praise throughout the session.

Under

(Moving round)

Using a large cloth, two people hold the cloth like a bridge. Sing (to the tune of 'Here we go round the mulberry bush'):

> We go <u>under</u> the cloth
> <u>under</u> the cloth
> <u>under</u> the cloth.
> We go <u>under</u> the cloth
> <u>under</u> we go.

As you sing, one person leads the children underneath the cloth behind each other in a line. The cloth is being held so that it just brushes their heads as they go underneath it. Sing twice, then put the large cloth away and sit in the circle with a <u>small</u> cloth on the floor in the middle of the circle.

Animals under

(Extending concept 'under' by using it)

Introduce a toy animal and say that he likes to sit on the cloth (model this) but sometimes he likes to sit under the cloth (model this). Ask one child individually to place the animal:

- on the cloth;
- under the cloth.

Next invite this child to choose someone else, and then to tell them to put the animal **under** or **on** the cloth. That child then chooses another and so on.

Feely bag shapes

(Categorisation)

Put a hoop and a shallow box mid-circle. Put a round shape in the hoop. Pass a feely bag which contains round and square shapes (same colour). Children select one shape from the bag. Help them to decide if it is round, and so goes in the circle hoop, or if it is **not** round and goes into the shallow box. Continue till all have had a turn.

Singing rhyme

Touch each part as it is sung.

> Heads, shoulders, knees and toes, knees and toes,
> Heads, shoulders, knees and toes, knees and toes,
> and eyes and ears and mouth and nose,
> Heads, shoulders, knees and toes.

Bodyparts

Adult calls out 'Can you touch your…?'

nose	*eyes*	*knees*	*toes*
eyebrows	*nose*	*eyes*	*ears*
teeth	*eyebrows*	*eyes*	*toes*
eyebrows	*nose*	*ears*	*teeth*

Closing round

(Cooperation to make something)

Give a large threading bead and brick to each person. Tell them to think a nice thought. Say we will gather our nice thoughts and keep them. Pass a string around for each person to add a brick to. Show what you have all made together. Display till next session.

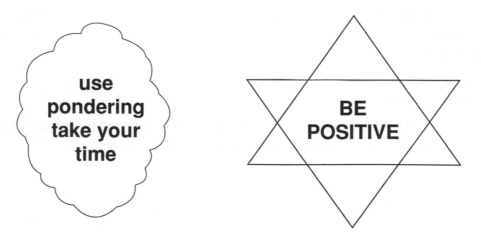

use
pondering
take your
time

BE
POSITIVE

Nursery Session 9

MATERIALS NEEDED
- Ball.
- Two animals and upturned box.
- Tube (as a spout) and spider.
- Threading beads (red and blue); one for each person.
- Piece of string to thread beads on.

Please keep language pace *slow* and *simple*. Use 'pondering' to slow your pace and invite shared thought. Praise throughout the session.

Roll the ball

Say your name and roll the ball to someone else in the group, e.g. 'My name is Jack.' (If the children are skilled in this they can say their name and who they will roll it to: 'My name is Tom and I will roll it to Angela.') Encourage children to say the sentence. Praise good sitting.

use praise phrases

On and under

(Putting 'on' and 'under' together again so that children will not lose one or the other concept as they might if they are presented too far apart)

Place an upturned box mid-circle. Tell the story of two animals playing hide and seek. Place one **on** or **under** the box. The other then looks for him.

Give the children the opportunity to place the animals **on** or **under** the box themselves as part of the hide and seek game.

Nursery rhyme (with actions)

(Awareness of rhyme/kinaesthetic involvement to aid memory)

(Standing)

Sing:

> Incy Wincy spider
> climbing up the spout,
> down came the rain
> and washed the spider out.
> Out came the sun
> and dried up all the rain,
> Incy Wincy spider
> Climbs up the spout again.

Ponder that some of the words sound the same: spout, out; rain, again.

Sing the rhyme again. Leave out the words 'out' and 'again', letting the children sing them. Comment that they remembered/sang the words 'out' and 'again', the word that sounds like 'rain'. (At this point you are first raising awareness of the way words can rhyme.)

Place a model spout (tube) in the circle. Ask children to choose whether to make him climb **up** to the top or **down** to the bottom and then to follow this choice with appropriate action.

(Sitting)

'Incy Wincy spider climbed **up** the spout to the top.' Model this. Then, 'Incy Wincy spider climbed **down** the spout to the bottom.' Model this.

Trains

(Children sit in a circle. Adults stand)

Explain that you are going to be the engine of the train. Go to each child and ask 'Will you join my train?' The child is encouraged to say 'Yes' or 'Yes I will' and they join on behind you. If a child refuses twice use your knowledge of that child to decide whether to pass on again or encourage to join in. When everyone is on the train, chug round then come to rest in a circle again.

Closing round

(Sequencing)

Give each child a threading bead in a sequence, e.g. *red, blue, red, blue, red, blue.* Say '*red*' or '*blue*' as you give the bead to a child. Pass the thread from person to person to add the beads. Comment on the pattern you have all made. Talk about the colours. Display with the other string from last session. Ask if anyone can remember the happy thought they had.

use
pondering
take your
time

BE
POSITIVE

Nursery Session 10

MATERIALS NEEDED

- Ball.
- Two animals and small box.
- Box large enough for a child to sit in.
- Two large pieces of card (on which to draw a face and body).
- <u>Plus</u> a pair of long arms <br> a pair of short arms <br> a pair of long legs <br> a pair of short legs <br> long hair <br> short hair. } Prepared cutouts to put on to the face and body
- Bear.

Please keep language pace *slow* and *simple*. Use 'pondering' to slow your pace and invite shared thought. Praise throughout the session.

Roll the ball

(Focusing in)

use pondering take your time

Say your name and roll the ball to someone else in the group, e.g. 'My name is Jack.' (If the children are skilled in this they can say their name and who they will roll it to: 'My name is Tom and I will roll it to Angela.') Encourage children to say the sentence. Praise good sitting.

On, under, behind

(Checking and extending use of concept words)

Use a story involving two animals playing hide and seek. Ask the children to hide an animal

on <br> under <br> in <br> behind } the box

Now using a <u>large box</u> invite children to play a game with one of the animals. The animal seeks and the child hides behind or inside the box. The child is encouraged to say where they are hiding. The rest of the group is asked where the child is hiding before the game begins.

Trains

(Turn-taking, cooperation, energising)

(Children sit in circle. Adult stands)

Explain that you are going to be the engine of the train. Go to each child and ask 'Will you join my train?' The child is encouraged to say 'Yes' or 'Yes I will' and they join on behind you. If a child refuses twice use your knowledge of that child to decide whether to pass on again or encourage to join in. When everyone is on the train, chug round then come to rest in a circle again.

Long and short

(Checking understanding and use of words 'long' and 'short')

On the two cards draw a face. Ask the children:

What do I need to draw: eyes, nose, mouth, ears, eyebrows?

Draw simple bodies. Show the children the cutouts you have made of the arms. Point out that two arms are long and two arms are short. Invite one child to place the long arms on a body. Then invite another child to place the short arms on a body. Repeat the process with the short legs and long legs. Show the long hair and short hair. Invite children to place the hair. The bodies may have a combination of long legs, short arms, long hair. Any combination is fine.

Go around the circle asking children to show you (by pointing) the:

long legs	short legs
short hair	long hair
long arms	short arms

BE
POSITIVE

Closing round

(Emotional warmth)

Bear hugs. Introduce a bear who wants hugs. Pass him round the circle to each child. Say how happy he is now they have hugged him.

use praise
phrases

Nursery Session 11

MATERIALS NEEDED

- Ball.
- Long piece of ribbon. Short piece of ribbon or tinsel (etc.). (Make them noticeably different.)
- Simple drawing or picture based on 'Twinkle twinkle little Star', such as a child sitting on a bed looking out of the window at the star (see Appendix).
- Two large pieces of card (on which to draw a face and body) and pencil.
- Large bunch of keys.
- Heavy object, such as a paperweight.

Please keep language pace *slow* and *simple*. Use 'pondering' to slow your pace and invite shared thought. Praise throughout the session.

Roll the ball

(Focusing in)

Say your name and roll the ball to someone else in the group, e.g. 'My name is Jack.' (If the children are skilled in this they can say their name and who they will roll it to: 'My name is Tom and I will roll it to Angela.') Encourage children to say the sentence. Praise good sitting.

use praise phrases

Long ribbon, short ribbon

(Extending awareness of concepts 'long'/'short')

Explain that you have a long ribbon and a short ribbon. Put them into the circle for comparison. 'Let's see how many people can hold the short ribbon.' Invite children one by one to stand up and hold it. Count how many people are holding it. Then they sit down. 'How many people can hold the long ribbon?' Repeat the process with the long ribbon.

Long snake, short snake

(As before)

'Let's make a short snake.' Some children hold the ribbon then walk round the circle saying 'ssssss'. They sit down. Repeat the process with a long 'snake'. Put the two ribbons down in the middle of the circle. Name them, then ask if children can tell you which is **long** and which is **short**.

Mummy's keys

(Sound of 'k'. Help to develop this sound, which can be difficult to form correctly in the back of the throat, especially for children who have dummies beyond a certain age.) Show the children a bunch of keys. Tell the story as follows:

> Mummy went to the shops to buy some food.
> She came home with a heavy bag of food.
> 'Oh good,' she thought, 'I am very tired but I will soon be home and have a nice cup of tea. That will make me happy.'
> She tried to unlock the door with her keys. But when she tried to open the door with her keys, it went 'k'. [Be careful to make the noise in the back of your throat. Remember not to say the letter name.]
> Mummy said, 'Oh dear, I don't know which one is the right key. I will have to try them all,' and she was a bit worried.
> Can you help mummy to try the keys and make her happy?

Put the bunch of keys in the middle of the circle. Ask a child to pretend to be Mum using the wrong key. Encourage them to make the sound 'k' as you did. Then each time, ask the group to make the sound together then ask another child to pretend to try a key. The child can then choose the next child to try the key. When you are satisfied that everyone has been involved, find the right key and open the door and let Mum have her cup of tea.

Talk lightly about Mum being pleased, relieved, happy when she found the right key.

Questions

(Extending children's expressive language)

Show a simple drawing of a child looking out of a window at the star. Give a copy to each child to hold. Ask 'What do you *see*?' Prompt questions can include:

> Is it a boy or girl?
> What is she/he doing?
> When is it? Night or day?

Conclude by praising for effort.

BE POSITIVE

Trains

(Turn-taking, energising)

(Standing up)

Explain that you are going to be the engine of the train. Go to each child and ask 'Will you join my train?' The child is encouraged to say 'Yes' or 'Yes I will' and they join on

30

behind you. If a child refuses twice, use your knowledge of that child to decide whether to pass on again or encourage to join in. When everyone is on the train, chug round then come to rest in a circle again.

Long and short

(Checking understanding and use of words 'long' and 'short')

On the two cards draw a face. Ask the children:

> What do I need to draw: eyes, nose, mouth, ears, eyebrows?

Having created nice faces, draw simple bodies. Pass these round the circle to each child, so each child has a turn. Ask them to draw long arms, then the next to draw long legs, the next short arms, then short legs, then short hair, then long hair. Place the drawings in the middle of the circle.

Go around the circle asking children to show you (by pointing) the:

long legs	short legs
short hair	long hair
long arms	short arms

Closing round

(Conceptual understanding of heavy)

Pass a heavy object, like a paperweight. Ponder on the way it feels. Emphasise heavy. Use the word for each person holding the object.

**use
pondering
take your
time**

Nursery Session 12

MATERIALS NEEDED

- Shell or interesting object.
- Feely bag of things we wear and don't wear, e.g. sock, shoe, scarf, tie, hat, shell, brick, pen, spoon.
- Hoop or circle of wool/string and shallow box.
- Picture of a person.
- Two animals and a box.
- Incy Wincy spider and a tube for a spout (e.g. cardboard tube).
- Threading beads (red and blue) and string.

Please keep language pace *slow* and *simple*. Use 'pondering' to slow your pace and invite shared thought. Praise throughout the session.

Round

(Trust, developing internal thought processes)

Pass a shell or interesting object round. When a child has the shell in her hand, she can say 'My name is...'

BE POSITIVE

Feely bag: things we wear

(Categorisation)

A feely bag containing things we wear (e.g. socks, shoe, tie, scarf, hat) and two objects not in that category (e.g. fir cone, brick). There should be one object for each person in the group. In the middle of the circle lay a hoop (or circle of wool or string) and a shallow box lid. Place a picture of a person in the hoop.

The feely bag is passed around. The first child takes an object out of the bag. The group decides if it is something we wear. If so it is placed in the hoop. If not it is put in the box lid.

Inside outside

Place a small house or box in the circle. Two animals take turns to go inside to keep warm or outside to get cool. Ask the children to choose an animal and place it inside or outside. Encourage children to choose verbally where to put the animal before they place it.

Top and bottom

(Awareness of rhyme)

(Standing)

use praise phrases

Sing with actions:

> Incy Wincy spider
> climbing up the spout,
> down came the rain
> and washed the spider out.
> Out came the sun
> and dried up all the rain,
> Incy Wincy spider
> Climbs up the spout again.

Ponder that some of the words sound the same: spout, out; rain, again.

Sing the rhyme again. Leave out the words 'out' and 'again', letting the children sing them. Comment that they remembered/sang the words 'out' and 'again', the word that sounds like 'rain'. (At this point you are first raising awareness of the way words can rhyme.)

(Sitting)

(Practical continued development, 'up'/'down')

'Incy Wincy spider climbed **up** the spout to the top.' Model this. Then, 'Incy Wincy spider climbed **down** the spout to the bottom.' Model this. Place a model spout (tube) in the circle. Ask children to make him climb up to the top or down to the bottom.

Closing round

(Sequencing, memory)

Give each child a threading bead in a sequence, e.g. *red, blue, red, blue, red, blue.* Say '*red*' or '*blue*' as you give the bead to a child. Pass the thread from person to person to add the beads. Comment on the pattern you have all made. Talk about the colours.

use pondering take your time

Sessions for Foundation/ Key Stage 1

Are listed at the start of each session. Most are readily available in school or are included in the Appendix.

For four of the activities we have used pictures from the Talkabout series and Pragmatics series from Black Sheep Press (tel: 01535 631346).

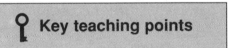

Twenty-five to 35 minutes depending on how long you wish to spend on each activity.

Key teaching points

Pace

Essential: keep *pace* and *content* of speech slow and uncluttered. Use **pondering** to wonder with the group about ideas that come out of the activities or to introduce new questions. For example, say 'Hmm, I have noticed that [pause] when you put Dozy Dog behind the tree [pause and consider] you were right. [pause] Hmm, but to me he looks as if he is in front of the tree? I wonder why that is? Shall we try it again?'

Thinking time

Give children at least 15 seconds' thinking time. Frame it positively by saying 'I can see you are thinking really well and carefully.' If the child cannot answer offer the help of the other children. The child retains control by choosing who they want to be helped by.

Positive praise phrases

Praise phrases should be going on all the time: 'good sitting', 'well done', 'brilliant listening', 'good, looking eyes and careful feet', 'good idea', 'thank you for listening so well to me', 'good thinking', 'you played that very well', 'I like your ideas'. Engage eye contact and smile, and also use accompanying low-key thumbs up gestures.

Try to avoid saying 'No, that's not right.' Clearly there are right and wrong answers but the group works on similar principles to brainstorming, where all ideas are listened to and considered, and then an answer is chosen from all the ideas. We tend to say 'Thank you, you spoke up really well. You gave me another idea.'

Language concepts: spirals of learning

The aim of the early sessions is to develop a structural basis to enable thinking skills and communication skills to develop, along with the confidence to formulate and express ideas and present those ideas to an audience.

The later sessions seek to consolidate this foundation and to build on it by extending vocabulary, expressive language, narrative and awareness of the structure of communication.

Responsive toys

Sometimes responsive toys are mentioned. If they are available they are useful tools to help children to realise that they must wait (e.g. until the toy resets itself) and sequence things in the right order (e.g. press teddy's paw, wait for beep, speak, press other paw) to ensure success.

Dynamic assessment

It will be clear from children's responses to activities whether they have grasped the concepts involved or not. This is a unique form of assessment, and can be ongoing. Concepts can be worked on in the classroom between sessions, then reassessed again in the next group session.

Fun

Enjoy this time together. It can be great fun, and fun is a powerful learning tool.

Main concepts covered in Foundation/ Key Stage 1 sessions

Session 1   Confidence building.
             Golden rules.

Session 2   Turn-taking.
             Identifying two feelings.
             Simple preferences and choices.

Session 3   Turn-taking.
             Position concepts.
             Visualisation, imagination and feelings.
             Sound recognition.

Session 4   Turn-taking.
             Positional concepts/adjectives.
             Effective eye contact.
             Visualisation (optional).

Session 5   Turn-taking.
             Listening.
             Positional concepts.
             Sound discrimination/decision-making.

Session 6   Turn-taking.
             Positional concepts.
             Giving effective eye contact.
             Sound discrimination.
             Feelings.

Session 7   Speaking to an audience.
             Turn-taking.
             Positional concepts.
             Generating ideas on a theme.
             Recall of events.
             Prediction.
             Feelings.
             Sound discrimination/decision-making.
             Eye contact (optional).

Session 8	Listening. Giving turns to others. Questioning. Recall. Sound discrimination. Listening and positional language. Categorisation.
Session 9	Listening. Waiting for a turn. Sound discrimination and decision-making. Listening and following instructions. Sound discrimination in words.
Session 10	Speaking to an audience. Generating ideas. Emotions/feelings: words, faces and gestures (non-verbal communication). Prediction. Imagination and categorisation. Recall.
Session 11	Listening for direction. Categorising and effective questioning. Verbal reasoning. Hypothesis checking. Feelings linked to behaviour. Turn-taking. Positive thinking and recall.
Session 12	Speed thinking. Sound discrimination. Positional language. Thinking about the needs of others. Listening (optional).

Foundation/KS1 Session 1

MATERIALS NEEDED
- Sheet of paper and a large felt-tip pen.
- Board to rest paper on and Blu-tack to secure it to a wall.
- Ball.

Say a little about how well children came in and joined you.

Opening round: name game

(Getting to know the group. Sitting down)

Tell the children you need to know their names so you will play a name game. Roll a ball across the circle a few times. Say your name and roll it to a child. They say their name and roll it to someone else and so on for several minutes until all have had a chance to roll the ball. Encourage them to say 'My name is . . .'

Recap on all the names.

Introduce the idea of the group working together for several sessions.

Fruit basket game

(Standing up)

Stand up in a circle. Adult walks around the circle and gives each child the name of a fruit (keep to three for simplicity). Thus: apple, orange, banana, apple, orange, banana. Include adults in this. Check children remember what fruit they are.

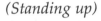

> Hands up apples. Hands up oranges. Hands up bananas. Sit down apples. Turn around oranges. Hop on one leg bananas. [And so on.]

> In a minute we are going to change places. I will say, apples change and all apples move to a new place in the circle. Then oranges will have a turn, then bananas. Now apples change.

Focus children on what you want by commenting on positive behaviour. Comment on children walking quietly and carefully across the circle.

> Oranges change.

Comment on positive behaviour in walking sensibly, taking care of other people in the circle, making space for someone, thinking about what they are doing. When playing this game in later sessions extend the language, e.g. 'Apples find a new place.'

> **fruit basket** (If ready for this level; if not leave until a future session). If you feel the group are ready you can play fruit basket. Explain that you will say **'fruit basket'** which means that everyone changes place at once. As before, comment on taking care of each other.

Golden Rules

(Sitting down)

Praise the group for having looked after each other in the last game by walking carefully and listening carefully and looking well.

Explain that the group will meet every week and that to make sure it is good fun for everyone in the group we will need to make sure that we take care of everyone in the group. Ask for ideas on how we can take care of each other in the circle, e.g. carefully listen to what people say, sit still.

Write down two or three with additional symbols, e.g. listening ear, careful feet. Put the sheet on the wall for future reference and add to it in future sessions.

Choose a name for the group. Use a voting system such as hands up and count preferences.

Changing Places

(Standing up)

'I want to change places with...'. (Name) changes places and this person then chooses someone else, saying 'I want to change places with...'. Encourage children to say the sentence but help children who find it difficult to speak out by allowing them to say just the name or point. Praise children who say the full sentence 'I want to change places with...'

Pass the sound   SSSSSSSSS

(Sitting down)

(Pass the sound how you would say it, not the letter name.)

'Pass' an 's' sound from your mouth on to your finger and on to the finger of the person next to you. The sound goes around to everyone. When it comes back to you, 'put it back' on your lips and stop the sound.

Sound snake

(Children sit in a circle. Adult stands)

Adult explains that they are all part of the sound snake. Go up to each child in the circle and say 'Would you join my sound snake?' Explain that as you made the 's' sound in the last game, you will all make the 's' sound as you go round and about the room being a snake.

Magic wink

(Eye contact)

Check that children can wink. If they cannot, use blinks instead of winks.

A child sits in a chair mid-circle. The group walks around watching closely. When the child winks at someone that person must wink back. If the chosen person does so, he or she can have a turn in the chair. Sing 'Here we go round the magic chair, who is she [he] going to pick?' to the tune of 'Here we go round the mulberry bush'.

Reverse the direction of the group after each person is chosen, to prevent dizziness.

Closing Round

(Standing)

Pass a smile. Put on sad faces then pass a smile round.

Foundation/KS1 Session 2

Remind the group of the chosen name of the group and refresh the golden rules.

Roll the ball

(Sitting down)

Say your name and roll the ball to someone else in the group, e.g. 'My name is Jack.' (If the children are skilled in this they can say their name and who they will roll it to: 'My name is Tom and I will roll it to Angela.') Encourage children to say the sentence, but don't insist.

Goldilocks

(Sitting down)

Identifying feelings

We will look at a story you may all know. Can you guess what it is by looking at the book's cover?

Recap the main points of the story of Goldilocks:

Goldilocks went into the three bears' cottage when they had gone for a walk.

She did some things they didn't like very much. She tasted their porridge and ate up all of baby bear's breakfast porridge. He was so hungry after his walk and feeling happy because he thought he was going to eat his bowl of porridge and yummy honey – but it had gone. And his chair was broken so he began to cry and tell his mum and dad how upset he was.

Then ask questions related to simple feelings in the story as follows:

Younger group

1 'When baby bear saw his empty porridge bowl, was he happy or sad?'
  Ask the children to choose a face from the middle of the circle to show how baby bear felt and hold it up.

Carry on to these questions if the group are coping easily.

2 'When daddy bear saw the broken chair was he happy or sad?'
3 'When mummy bear saw that baby bear's chair was broken was she happy or sad?'

Talk with children about their ideas. Point out different points of view, e.g. baby bear might be happy that his porridge had gone if he didn't like porridge.

Older group

Do as above but use the story of 'Jack and the beanstalk'. 'How did the giant feel when Jack took his things away?'

Waiting game

(Sitting very briefly)

Introduce this. 'When you see me do this – fold my arms and sit up straight – I am playing the waiting game. See how quickly you can play it.' Praise children for quickness. If a child is slow to join in try to hold on for a while as peer pressure often encourages them to after a while.

Circle train

(Standing and moving around to regather energies)

An 'engine' is chosen and the circle chugs round after him or her for a few circuits.

Fruit basket game

(Standing up)

Play once or twice to energise and focus the group.

Stand up in a circle. An adult walks around the circle and gives each child the name of a fruit (keep to three for simplicity), thus: apple, orange, banana, apple, orange etc. Include adults in this. Check children remember what fruit they are.

Hands up apples. Hands up oranges. Hands up bananas.

Sit down apples. Sit down oranges. Turn round bananas. Stand up apples. Turn round oranges. Stand up oranges.

In a minute we are going to change places. I will say, apples change and all apples move to a new place in the circle. Then oranges will have a turn, then bananas. Now apples change. Now oranges change. Now bananas change.

Focus children on what you want by commenting on positive behaviour. Comment on children walking quietly and carefully across the circle.

Waiting game

(To gather attention)

'Let me see if anyone notices and remembers how to play it.' Praise response.

I like this one best

With two model animals, talk about which one you like and why. 'I have a tiger and an elephant. I like the elephant because he is big.' Pass the two animals to the next person and ask 'Which animal do you like best?' Ask children if they can remember, for example, what John liked and why and repeat for several children.

Closing round: pass a smile

'Show me a sad face. We will try to change them to happy faces. Watch the smile go around the circle. Pass a smile.'

Foundation/KS1 Session 3

MATERIALS NEEDED

- Ball.
- Dozy Dog and houses/trees.
- Two sound cards for the sound train.
- Tambourine.
- Skipping rope.
- Feely bag with objects/pictures of the '*at*' family of words, e.g. cat, bat.

Roll the ball

(Standing up)

Ball roll: 'My name is . . . , I am going to roll the ball to . . .'

Waiting game

(Sitting down)

Play this to see if anyone remembers how to play. Praise responses.

Tambourine game

(Standing up)

Pass the tambourine round the circle calling '*in front*' or '*behind*'. The children pass the tambourine in front of themselves or behind their backs, then call '*shake*' and the child holding the tambourine shakes it. Children can take a turn to call '*in front*' or '*behind*'. If there is time trying this sitting down.

Dozy Dog

Choose a toy or plastic model of a dog to play the part of Dozy Dog. Trees (to scale) can be plastic or cut out of card. Houses can be made from two wooden blocks, or boxes, or small dolls house.

(Positional concepts; relative to position)

Ask for the dog to be put under a tree or house, then ask 'Where's dozy dog?' When children answer that he is under the tree, ask if he is on the carpet. Some children will have difficulty with seeing that two concepts can be held simultaneously and will often say he is under the tree. Explore this with the children with more examples, for example he can be on the carpet, under the box, next to Sarah etc.

Rhyme game

Pass round a feely bag with objects/pictures that rhyme with **cat** (i.e. from the 'at' family of words), i.e.

> bat   (use both creature and sports equipment)
> rat
> mat
> hat

You will need to duplicate these so each one has a card.

Children name it as they take it out of the bag and place it in the middle of the circle. Then cover them with a cloth and ask the children if they can remember the things under the cloth.

Ponder that you have noticed that all the words sound the same and you think that's interesting. Explore this with the children. Tell the children that another name for words sounding the same is that they rhyme. Highlight the double meaning of the word 'bat' and ask if there are any other words they can think of, e.g. fat, sat.

Imaginary animal

(Standing up)

Out of an imaginary box take an imaginary mouse or hamster – describe it, stroke its fur. Carefully pass it round the circle. Talk about how it may feel: scared, frightened, excited. Invite thoughts.

Optional

(Standing up)

Place a skipping rope in a circle. Children hold hands and on instructions jump as a group *in front of or behind* the rope circle.

(Thanks to Andrew Burnett, Chief Speech and Language Therapist for this good activity idea)

Sound snake

(Standing up)

(Remember: make the sound, not the name of the letter.)

A chosen child holds the chosen card, e.g. 's' and walks round the circle making that sound. They stand in front of another person in the group and say 'Will you join my S snake?' The person replies 'Yes, I will join your S snake' and walks behind the leader round the circle. The leader invites people to join the sound snake until everyone is involved. The leader chooses the person to be the next leader.

Closing round

(Standing up)

'Show me a sad face. We will try to change them to happy faces. Watch the smile go around the circle. Pass a smile.'

Foundation/KS1 Session 4

MATERIALS NEEDED

- Ball.
- Two toy animals: elephant and giraffe.
- Empty box just smaller than the giraffe standing up (a cut off cereal box is a good idea).
- Box.
- Chair.

Roll the ball

(Sitting down)

The child says his or her own name and rolls the ball. 'My name is...' The child says the name of the child he or she is rolling it to. 'I am rolling the ball to . . .'

Animal story

(Sitting down)

Use a box that is just too small for the giraffe to hide in unless lying down. *(A cut down cereal box is perfect.)*

Elmer the Elephant, wants to play hide and seek with Gerald Giraffe. He finds a box and plays a game. Elmer hides **on** the box. Gerald looks for him. Then **in** and **under**. Bring in '**behind**'.

Elmer Elephant, Elmer Elephant, where are you?

Facilitator models this two or three times, saying 'Where is he hiding?' Encourage the children to chant 'Elmer Elephant, Elmer Elephant, where are you?' Eventually Gerald discovers Elmer. The children are then invited to choose Elmer or Gerald.

Pass Option: Children may pass but are then given a chance to join in if they change their mind before the game finishes.

Talk about: <u>Tall</u> Gerald Giraffe being unable to hide behind the <u>small</u> box. Is Elmer as tall or smaller/shorter?

Magic wink

(Eye contact)

Check that children can wink. If they cannot, use blinks instead of winks.

A child sits in a chair mid-circle. The group walks around watching closely. When the child winks at someone that person must wink back. If the chosen person does so, he or she can have a turn in the chair. Sing 'Here we go round the magic chair, who is she [he] going to pick?' to the tune of 'Here we go round the mulberry bush'.

Reverse the direction of the group after each person is chosen, to prevent dizziness.

Sound train (s/sh)

(Standing up)

The adult explains that she is the engine of the train as they stand in the circle. Call each child by name to join on to the train. Explain that as you made the '*s*' sound before you will all make the '*sh*' sound as you go round and about the room being a train.

Closing round: Pass a smile

(Standing up)

Encourage children to model a sad face. Then pass a smile round encouraging eye contact and a happy face.

Additional optional activity

(Standing up)

Introduce the idea of an imaginary animal. 'See' its whiskers and little feet, smooth its fur. Pass it round the circle then put it back in its imaginary box.

Foundation/KS1 Session 5

MATERIALS NEEDED

- Ball.
- Empty box and two toy animals.
- Big bunch of keys.
- Dozy dog, trees and houses.

Introduction

Recap the purpose of the group.

Roll the ball

'My name is…I am rolling the ball to…'

Dragons keys

(Sitting down)

Theme listening (need a big jangly bunch of keys). Tell the dragon's story:

> Once there was a village where the people had lots of food to store but nowhere to put it. They asked the dragon who lived in a cave on the hill if they could put their food in his cave. He said yes – he would lock it into his cave with his big bunch of keys. [Show keys.]
>
> But if he was asleep when the villagers came he would get very cross if he was woken up and would roar. He suggested that if he was asleep the villagers should try to take away the keys without waking him.

Explain that the dragon will sit in the middle of the circle with eyes closed and the keys beside him or her. Then a villager could try to take the keys away from the dragon without jangling them. If the dragon hears the keys he wakes up and roars.

Choose a dragon and ask to hear their roar. They close their eyes in the middle of the circle sitting down and the keys put in front of them. Then choose a villager to take the keys away.

The dragon chooses the next dragon.

The villager chooses the next villager by pointing when the dragon's eyes are closed.

Fruit basket game

(Standing up)

Play once or twice to energise and focus the group.

Stand up in a circle. An adult walks around the circle and gives each child the name of a fruit (keep to three for simplicity). Thus: apple, orange, banana, apple, orange etc. Include adults in this. Check that children remember what fruit they are.

Hands up apples. Hands up oranges. Hands up bananas.

In a minute we are going to change places. I will say, apples change and all apples move to a new place in the circle. Then oranges will have a turn, then bananas. Now apples change. Now oranges change. Now bananas change.

Focus children on what you want by commenting on positive behaviour. Comment on children walking quietly and carefully across the circle.

Dozy Dog

(Positional concepts; relative to position)

Dozy Dog is placed behind or in front of buildings, houses and trees. Children take turns to do this and say whether the dog is in front or behind.

Closing round: Pass a smile

(Standing up)

'Show me a sad face. We will try to change them to happy faces. Watch the smile go around the circle. Pass a smile.'

Foundation/KS1 Session 6

> ## MATERIALS NEEDED
> - Ball.
> - Feely bag and pictures of things in the 'in' family, e.g. tin, pin.

Ball roll

The child says his or her own name and the name of person the ball is rolled to.

Rhyme game

Pass round a feely bag with objects/pictures of things that rhyme with tin (i.e. from the 'in' family of words), i.e.

> tin
> bin
> pin

You will need to duplicate these so each child has a card or object.

Children name the item as they take it out of the bag and place it in the middle of the circle. Then cover the items with a cloth and ask the children if they can remember the things under the cloth.

Ponder that you have noticed all the words sound the same and you think that's interesting. Explore this with the children. Tell the children that another name for words sounding the same is that they rhyme. Ask if there are any other words they can think of, e.g. fin, chin.

People in the middle

(Standing up)

Three children stand up and are asked in turn to put themselves in the middle of the three. Choose another three children. When all have had a turn change the instructions to:

[*Name*] stand behind [*name*].

[*Name*] stand between [*name*] and [*name*].

[*Name*] stand in front of [*name*].

Optional

If appropriate, choose five children and ask the group:

- Who is in the middle?
- Can Tom put himself in the middle?
- If George is at the beginning/front who is at the end of the line?
- Can George stand next to Claire?
- Can Claire stand between Sarah and Sophie?

Clapping game

Ask children to clap their first name as they go round in the circle.

Round

Happy. I feel happy when...

Talk about what makes us happy. Ask children to fold their arms and when they have an idea to keep it in. Go round the circle and ask for their ideas. Wait a while but if children appear not to have an idea give a few general ideas and see if they accept them. Go round the circle: 'I feel happy when...'

Closing round: Pass a smile

(Standing up)

'Show me a sad face. We will try to change them to happy faces. Watch the smile go around the circle. Pass a smile.'

Foundation/KS1 Session 7

MATERIALS NEEDED
- Shell or (interesting object).
- Dozy Dog, Annie, village (trees, houses).
- Two hoops or circles of card.
- Objects in a feely bag with initial sounds 's' and 'p'.
- Pictures of Annie feeling happy, angry, sad, shocked (in Appendix).

Opening round: pass the shell

Model holding the shell (or other interesting object) at arm's length, and looking at the person opposite you, say your <u>own</u> name. Pass it on to the person next to you and show them how to do this. Pass it on to one more person and explain it to them.

Then take the shell back and check that all the children understand what to do. Model it once more. Say how difficult it can be not to say the name of the person you are looking at (this is quite likely to happen with some children), then say your own name and pass the shell around.

Praise the group then pass the shell round once more.

Annie and Dozy Dog

(Predictions and feelings)

(Sitting down)

Part I

> Annie is taking Dozy Dog for a walk. He is being very naughty. He runs away from her and hides. 'Dozy Dog! Dozy Dog! Where are you?' she calls. Can you hide Dozy dog so that Annie can't see him?

Give the children the opportunity to hide Dozy Dog and say whether he is behind, in front of, between or next to an object in the village.

Part II

(Moving on to prediction)

Tell the story of Annie taking Dozy out for another walk, when he runs away again.

> **Where do you think he went? What do you think he did?**

Gather ideas from the children. Choose one idea and develop it, e.g. Dozy Dog went into the village shop.

What do you think he did? What do you think happened?

Gather ideas and choose one to develop, e.g. 'Yes, he ran into the shop and found some packets of crisps and bit one.'

What do you think happened?

Eventually Annie comes round the corner and sees Dozy Dog.

What do you think she <u>felt</u> when she saw him?

Ask children to choose between pictures of Annie looking happy, shocked, sad, angry.

Pairwork

Talk to the person next to you for a minute. Collect ideas. What do you think Annie did when she saw Dozy Dog?

Collect ideas and encourage discussion of feelings involving angry, worried, relieved, embarrassed. Include real memories of children getting lost and parents' reactions.

Magic wink

(Eye contact)

Check that children can wink. If they cannot, use blinks instead of winks.

A child sits in a chair mid-circle. The group walks around watching closely. When the child winks at someone that person must wink back. If the chosen person does so, he or she can have a turn in the chair. Sing 'Here we go round the magic chair, who is she [he] going to pick?' to the tune of 'Here we go round the mulberry bush'.

Reverse the direction of the group after each person is chosen, to prevent dizziness.

Sound hoops ('*s*'/'*p*')

(Sitting down)

Use a feely bag containing objects that begin with '*s*' and '*p*', e.g.

sock	peg	
soap	pen	
seal	pin	
saucer	pig	
sand	potato	
sticky tape	pants	

Note: at this stage don't include words that include a double consonant, e.g. '*st*', '*sn*', '*sp*', '*pl*', '*pr*'.

Put same-coloured (preferably neutral) hoops down on the floor with '*s*' and '*p*' cards in them. Invite the children to select an object from the feely bag and guess what it is by feeling it, then take it out, identifying the initial sound. The child places the object in the correct sound hoop – with help and guidance as needed.

When all have had a turn, sit down and invite the children to remember who had what item and what it began with. Begin by asking each child what they had and what it began with. Then ask children if they can remember what particular children had.

Sound snake

(Standing up)

A child chooses and holds a card, e.g. '*s*', and walks round the circle making that sound. He or she stands in front of another person in the group and says 'Will you join my s snake?' The person replies, 'Yes, I will join your s snake', and walks behind the leader round the circle. The leader invites people to join the sound snake until everyone is involved.

The leader chooses a person to be the next leader.

Closing round

Talk briefly about what a wish is. Pass a star or wand. 'I wish that . . . I wish for . . .'

Foundation/KS1 Session 8

MATERIALS NEEDED

- Responsive toy, e.g. parrot which records voice then plays back, *or* shell.
- Skipping rope (optional).
- Story picture of Annie on beach (3 or 4 copies).
- Toni's balloons (see Appendix).
- Blu-tack to attach balloons to question board.
- Cut out question circles (see Appendix). Colour code as shown below.

Opening round

(Sitting down)

Say hello to the parrot. If the parrot does not repeat the child's name, make it clear that it is something the *parrot* has not done.

Alternatively, pass the shell and say your name to the person opposite you.

Toni's balloons

Pin the picture from Appendix on board or side of a box beside you so it can be easily seen by the group. Make sure it is enlarged to A3 at least.

Place the cut-out question circles (coloured) In front of you.

> who? – blue
> did what? – yellow
> when? – red
> where? – green
> how? ⎫
> why? ⎭ white

Tell the children that Toni wants lots of coloured balloons and that they are going to help by 'talking about the picture'.

Distribute the pictures of Annie and Dozy Dog on the beach (Appendix). Give each child a copy or share between two. Say this is today's picture story. Let the children look at the picture and discuss it in pairs. Ask them to tell you about the picture story.

Accept what the children tell you and put the coloured balloons up with Blu-tack on the picture of Toni's balloons, according to what they tell you. For example, if they say 'dog chasing cat' put up 'who' balloon (blue) and also 'did what' balloon (yellow) and give them lots of praise. Then ask them 'where' is this happening? (on the beach), and put up green balloon when they give you an answer. Then ask, Can any of you tell me *when* this happened? Can you look carefully and see? (night or day). If they give you an appropriate answer put up the red balloon (when). Summarise by retelling the story they have given you with as many details as they have given you.

Put away the circles and board for another time.

Behind and in front

(Standing up)

Place a skipping rope in a circle. Children hold hands and on instructions jump as a group <u>in front/behind</u> the rope circle.

Closing round: pass the sound ('*sh*')

(Standing up)

Stand up in a circle. Make a '*sh*' (or other chosen) sound, put your finger to your lips and 'take' the sound on to your finger, passing it to the next person who is holding out a finger to receive it. The sound is 'passed' from finger to finger round the circle, until it returns to you, who then take it back to your lips and stop the sound.

Foundation/KS1 Session 9

MATERIALS NEEDED

- Ball or responsive toy.
- Two cards for the sound snake: 's', 'f'.
- Pragmatics pictures of frightened boy and some related situations (available from Black Sheep Press).

Opening round

'My name is . . .' use parrot or responsive toy, or roll the ball.

Sound snake (*s, f*)

(Standing up. Play level I once to remind children about the game)

Level I

A child is chosen as the snake leader and holding the '*s*' card, walks round the circle making the '*s*' sound. She asks people in the circle 'Will you join my sound snake?' They say 'Yes, I'd like to join your sound snake', and slither round at the end of the line of people in the snake.

At the end the snake forms a circle and then stops ready for the next game.

Level II

Allow each child to choose from a box of objects beginning with '*s*' or '*f*', and hold on to it for the game which follows. Then, give an *s* card to one child (a) and give an '*f*' card to another child (b). Child (a) then goes around the circle asking 'Will you join my '*s*' sound snake?' If the child in the circle has an object that begins with '*s*' they say 'Yes, I can join your sound snake because I have a *sack*.' But if they haven't they say 'No, I can't join your sound snake because I have a *feather*.' When all the '*s*' people are collected the snake goes back to the beginning.

Child (b), the '*f*' person, then goes around the circle in the same way, collecting people with objects beginning with '*f*'.

Listening to the tambourine

(Sitting down)

The task is to pass the tambourine round the circle as soundlessly as possible. The children close their eyes and pass the tambourine. The facilitator walks round the circle behind the children and after a while touches a child who has the tambourine on the shoulder. This child shakes the tambourine. The rest of the group have to keep their eyes closed and point to where they think the sound is coming from. Open eyes and check if they were right. Praise well for playing well.

Feelings

Ask the children, 'When we play the game well, how do we feel?' Then talk about what happens when things don't go well. Talk about 'frightened'. Show the corresponding faces from the Pragmatics pack (or another source) and the related situations.

Talk about your own experiences of being frightened and then ask the children for their experiences. In the end, emphasise that it is OK to be frightened.

Sound game

This is rather like the fruit basket game. Give each person in the group a sound to remember. Use 'p', 's', 'k' (remember to use the sound, not the name of the letter). Encourage the children to say the sound that they are. Then call instructions such as

'p' hop three times.
'k' turn around twice.

Then introduce positional concepts (next to, in front of):

's' stand next to me.
'p' stand in front of Mrs James.
'k' stand in front of the door.
's' stand next to the table.

If children feel confident with this, ask one of the children to take over calling the instructions.

Closing round

(Standing up)

Say 'Put your sad faces on and let's see if we can cheer them up with a smile.'

Foundation/KS1 Session 10

MATERIALS NEEDED

- Object to pass.
- Mr Bear's honeypot with animal inside.
- Mr Bear's question cards.

Opening round: pass the object

(Getting to know the group. Sitting down)

The facilitator models holding an object out in front of her, looking at the person opposite and saying their name clearly and confidently (twice around the circle). Say how difficult you might find it to look at someone and say your own name.

Mr Bear's honeypot

Play once.

Tell a story of a bear who likes to play a game with the animals in the forest by hiding a creature in his pot. The group ask Mr Bear questions and Mr Bear answers them. (When someone guesses the object correctly Mr Bear shows the group what is in the pot.) 'And Mr Bear [a puppet] is going to help you. Get into pairs and think of some questions to ask Mr Bear.' (Use Mr Bear as a puppet. The children ask him directly and he answers them. When all the children have been asked, use the following as an extension.)

Lay out the five question cards. Say to the children that you have some ideas for questions that would be good to ask.

> Where does it live?
> How does it move?
> How many legs?
> What does it have on its body?
> What colour is it?

Encourage the children in pairs to choose the question they want to ask. When a question has been asked, e.g. 'What colour is it?' put that question card on to the honey pot to show it has been asked. If that question is asked again, point out that it has already been asked and is on the pot. Carry on until they guess what it is.

Sound work

(Play standing up and crossing the circle if movement is needed at this stage)

Pass a sound *(draw attention to the length of sounds, 'ss' being a long sound).*

The facilitator makes the sound, e.g. 'SSSSsss', and 'takes the sound' from her mouth to their forefinger. She then 'passes' the sound to another person in the circle. Once this person's finger is touched he or she starts to make the sound and passes it on by touching someone else's finger.

Make a pincer shape with your forefinger and thumb and explain that now you will pass a <u>short</u> sound round the circle.

- Pass '*p*' round two and three times then 'catch' the sound, when it 'disappears'.
- Pass another short sound (children can choose '*k*').

Pass the pretend box

(Sitting down. Imagination and categorisation)

'I have a . . . in my box.' This can be previously discussed with the group in terms of category, e.g. 'This is a fruit box. So what could you have in your box (e.g. apples, pears, etc.)?' Then play the game using these ideas. 'This is my fruit box. I have a pear in it.' Extend this using different categories, colour, even numbers, animals, depending on the needs of the group.

Closing round

'My favourite circle game is . . .'

Foundation/KS1 Session 11

MATERIALS NEEDED

- Ball.
- Dozy Dog, Annie, trees and houses, model tiger.
- Mr Bear, honeypot, creature to hide in the honeypot, question cards.
- Optional: objects with initial sounds 's' and 'p'.

Opening round: roll the ball

(Sitting down)

Close your eyes and roll the ball. The person to whom it rolls says his or her name.

Dozy Dog gets lost

(Generates feelings)

Tell a story of Dozy Dog sneaking out of the house one morning and going for a walk by himself. He soon realises that he is lost. He runs this way and that. He becomes hungry and cold. Explore: what he may be feeling; what Annie may be feeling. Use houses, trees and tiger as props to stimulate imagination.

Move on to him being found by Annie. Explore: what both are feeling; how this may change.

Discuss

- What effects this is likely to have on their future behaviour.
- Will Annie trust him so much? Will she keep the doors locked?
- Will Dozy Dog be careful not to go out without Annie or will he forget how horrible he felt and do it again?

Changing places

(Sitting down. The rule is choose someone who hasn't had a turn)

Talk in pairs. Talk about ways to move, e.g. hop, jump, roll, skip. Then in the circle each person decides on a way to move across the circle.

Choose two people. Check how they will be moving across the circle, e.g. person (a) will hop, person (b) will jump. Ask them to change places with each other using their chosen movement.

Pass the sound

(Standing up)

'Pass' an '*s*' sound from your mouth on to your finger and on to the finger of the person next to you. The sound goes round to everyone. When it comes back to you 'put it back' on your lips and stop the sound. Pass '*s*' first.

Pass a long sound, e.g. '*Sh...*' from your mouth to your forefinger. Then 'pass' the sound to another person in the circle. Once their finger is touched they start to make the sound and pass it on by touching someone else's finger.

Make a pincer shape with your forefinger and thumb and explain that now you will pass a <u>short</u> sound round the circle.

- Pass '*t*' round two or three times then 'catch' the sound, when it 'disappears'
- Pass another short sound, e.g. '*d*', '*k*'.

Close by 'catching' the sound in your hand.

Sound hoops (optional)

If time is available, Use a feely bag containing objects that begin with '*s*' and '*p*', e.g.

sock	peg
soap	pen
seal	pin
saucer	pig
sand	potato
sticky tape	pants

Note: at this stage don't include words that include a double consonant, e.g. '*st*', '*sn*', '*sp*', '*pl*', '*pr*'.

Put same-coloured (preferably neutral) hoops down on the floor with '*s*' and '*p*' cards in them. Invite the children to select an object from the feely bag and guess what it is by feeling it, then take it out, identifying the initial sound. The child places the object in the correct sound hoop – with help and guidance as needed.

Closing round

'The best thing about the circle today was...'

Foundation/KS1 Session 12

MATERIALS NEEDED

- Two 'slices of bread' (can be plastic, box lids or wooden shapes).
- 'Filling': box of objects (of pictures beginning with 'f' and 'sh').
- Optional: bunch of keys, if Dragon keys is played.

Opening round: roll the ball

(Getting to know the group. Sitting down)

Say your name and roll the ball to someone else in the group: 'and my favourite is . . .'
Talk about who can remember what Susie liked best.

Pointing game

(Standing up or sitting down)

Try pointing to another person in the circle, look at them and say your own name. Speed up to go as fast as you can. It can be quite difficult to maintain. Encourage the children to be very comfortable with making mistakes and to enjoy the game.

Silly sandwiches

(Sitting down)

Ask, 'What is your favourite sandwich?' Tell the children to talk in pairs. 'Let's make some silly sandwiches.'

Encourage each child to choose an object or picture beginning with 'sh' or 'f' from the box to put in between the 'slices of bread' and say, e.g.

I have made a 'shoe' sandwich

I have made a 'fish' sandwich

I have made a 'sugar' sandwich.

Then pass the bread on to the next person. At the end of the game put 'f' and 'sh' cards in the middle of the circle and ask children to put their object on the card with the same initial sound.

People in the middle

(Standing up)

Three children stand up and are asked in turn to put themselves in the middle of the three. Introduce the idea that another word for middle is **in between**.

Choose another three children. When all have had a turn change the instructions to:

[*Name*] stand behind [*name*].
[*Name*] stand between [*name*] and [*name*].
[*Name*] stand in front of [*name*].

If appropriate, choose five children and ask the group:

Who is in the middle?
Can Tom put himself in the middle?
If George is at the beginning/front, who is at the end of the line?

Circle train

(To focus the group. Standing up)

Stand in a circle. Choose a leader to chug around the room followed by the rest of the group. End in a big circle.

Closing round

Pass a wand, a star, or a 'wishing stone'. Take one wish round the circle. 'A wish for myself...I wish...' Take a second wish round the circle. 'A wish for someone else...I wish...'

Optional

If more listening work is needed, substitute Dragon's keys for the Pointing game and leave out the Circle train if time is short.

Sessions for Key Stage 2

Materials	

Are listed at the start of each session. Most are readily available in school or are included in the Appendix.

For four of the activities we have used pictures from the Talkabout series and Pragmatics series from Black Sheep Press (tel: 01535 631346).

Twenty-five to 35 minutes depending on how long you wish to spend on each activity.

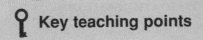

Pace

Essential: keep *pace* and *content* of speech slow and uncluttered. Use **pondering** to wonder with the group about ideas that come out of the activities or to introduce new questions. For example, say 'Hmm, I have noticed that [pause] when you put Dozy Dog behind the tree [pause and consider] you were right. [pause] Hmm, but to me he looks as if he is in front of the tree? I wonder why that is? Shall we try it again?'

Thinking time

Give children at least 15 seconds' thinking time. Frame it positively by saying 'I can see you are thinking really well and carefully.' If the child cannot answer offer the help of the other children. The child retains control by choosing who they want to be helped by.

Positive praise phrases

Praise phrases should be going on all the time: 'good sitting', 'well done', 'brilliant listening', 'good, looking eyes and careful feet', 'good idea', 'thank you for listening so well to me', 'good thinking', 'you played that very well', 'I like your ideas'. Engage eye contact and smile, and also use accompanying low-key thumbs up gestures.

Try to avoid saying 'No, that's not right.' Clearly there are right and wrong answers but the group works on similar principles to brainstorming, where all ideas are listened to and considered, and then an answer is chosen from all the ideas. We tend to say 'Thank you, you spoke up really well. You gave me another idea.'

Language concepts: spirals of learning

The aim of the early sessions is to develop a structural basis to enable thinking skills and communication skills to develop, along with the confidence to formulate and express ideas and present those ideas to an audience.

The later sessions seek to consolidate this foundation and to build on it by extending vocabulary, expressive language, narrative and awareness of the structure of communication.

Responsive toys

Sometimes responsive toys are mentioned. If they are available they are useful tools to help children to realise that they must wait (e.g. until the toy resets itself) and sequence things in the right order (e.g. press teddy's paw, wait for beep, speak, press other paw) to ensure success.

Dynamic assessment

It will be clear from children's responses to activities whether they have grasped the concepts involved or not. This is a unique form of assessment, and can be ongoing. Concepts can be worked on in the classroom between sessions, then reassessed again in the next group session.

Fun

Enjoy this time together. It can be great fun, and fun is a powerful learning tool.

Main concepts covered in Key Stage 2 sessions

Session 13   Turn-taking, focusing.
Awareness of syllables.
Encouraging creative narrative skills and extending doing words.
Familiarising children with word families which rhyme.
Memory.

Session 14   Turn-taking, focusing.
Awareness of syllables.
Encouraging creative narrative skills and extending doing words.
Familiarising children with word families which rhyme.
Memory.
Positive non-verbal communication (NVC).

Session 15   Turn-taking, focusing with positive emotions.
Developing narrative skills and vocabulary.
Familiarising children with word families which rhyme.
Sound production and discrimination: 'ch' and 'f'.
Positive NVC.

Session 16   Turn-taking, focusing with positive emotions.
Awareness of syllables.
Listening for a purpose, problem-solving.
Developing narrative skills and vocabulary.
Positive NVC.

Session 17   Turn-taking, focusing. Recall.
Exploring a variety of feelings through discussion.
Group decision-making.
Familiarising children with word families which rhyme.
Talking in pairs, reporting back.
Positive NVC.

Session 18   Sound production: 's'.
              Recall from last session on feelings.
              Listening for a purpose.
              Positional vocabulary.
              Awareness of syllables.
              Thinking positively for self and others.

Session 19   Awareness of syllables.
              Visualisation to aid recall.
              Developing awareness of categories when forming questions.
              Maintaining attention with eye contact.
              Feelings; worried.
              Positive NVC.

Session 20   Maintaining attention with eye contact.
              Listening. Turn-taking.
              Feelings and actions.
              Familiarising children with word families which rhyme.
              Preferences.

Session 21   Listening for a purpose.
              Awareness of syllables.
              Discrimination task using rhyme.
              Positive NVC.

Session 22   Relating facial cues to emotion.
              Developing concentration.
              Feelings: positive/negative. Outcomes.
              Maintaining attention with eye contact.
              Awareness of syllables.

Session 23   Extending conversation.
              Creative narrative skills. Feelings/moods.
              Maintaining attention with eye contact.
              Discussion of feelings (bored/scared) linked to actions and outcomes.
              Discrimination task using rhyme.
              Sound production and discrimination: 'ch', 'sh'.

Session 24   Asking questions about feelings.
              Awareness of syllables.
              Developing categories when forming questions.
              Talk about feelings: worried.
              Discussing alternative strategies.

KS2 Session 13

MATERIALS NEEDED
- Ball.
- Pictures of spider, bed, tree, table, television, chair, window, carpet, snake (as in Appendix), cut out individually.
- Cards showing objects in the '*at*' family (cat, hat, rat etc.) and also in the '*ouse*' family (mouse, house).

Roll the ball (to focus)

Roll the ball to each other in the circle, taking turns. As you hold the ball you say 'My favourite colour is...'

Clapping our names (syllable clap)

(Sit or stand)

Model clapping the syllables in the first name of the group. An adult goes around the circle clapping the first names, e.g.

Tom - my,	Claire,	Chris-to-pher
Clap/clap,	clap,	clap/clap/clap

Now ask the children to clap their name in turns round the circle.

Stage 2. If they are proficient at this go around again clapping their first name and surname.

Storylines

(Encouraging creative narrative skills and extend 'doing' words)

(Sitting down)

Lay out the picture cards on the floor in the middle of the circle, keeping back the spider. An adult uses the spider in a sequence of activities with the objects. For example, the spider runs up the tree, creeps on to the bed, tickles mouse and then hides under the table so that teddy can't see him.

Emphasise that a good story needs an <u>ending</u>. Encourage one child to hold the spider and sit in the middle of the circle with the visual prompts ready to play the game. Ask for ideas from the group as to what they think the spider interacts with each object. The child chooses one and acts it out with the pictures. Depending on time and need, encourage several children to do this.

Go around the circle asking each child (and adult) in turn to show you a 'story' using the spider with 'doing words' or 'verbs'.

Rhyme game

(Sitting down initially)

First familiarise children with the words prior to their recognising rhyming words).

Give out cards depicting objects ending in '*at*' or '*ouse*' (bat, cat, mouse), one to each person in the group. Help the children to identify the word linked to their picture then play the game by saying 'Stand up mouse, stand up bat, stand up cat, sit down mouse, stand up house, sit down bat' and so on.

Rhyme train

(Using the same visual prompt cards)

(Standing up in a circle)

Explain the game: 'This is my rhyme train. If your word sounds like mine, rhymes, then you can join my train when I ask you.'

Go around the circle showing and saying your word, e.g. 'Cat, will you join my sound train?' Help the children to decide if their word sounds like 'cat' and if so they join on your train behind you as you carry on round the circle.

Play the game using a word from the other family of words to include the other children.

Closing games

Round: 'What I liked best in our circle today.'

Round: 'Can you remember how to clap your name round the circle?'

KS2 Session 14

Clapping game

(Sitting down)

Go around the circle. Each person claps their first and last name while they say it.

Guess the name

(Watch for children who confuse phonic sounding out with syllables, e.g. T-o-mm-y as opposed to Tom-my.)

An adult claps the first name of a child without saying it. The task of the group is to guess whose name it is. For example, if the name is 'Robin' talk about it having two syllables or claps. Some children have names with one syllable or clap, so it can't be their name. Some children have three syllables or claps so it can't be them. If the children cannot work it out begin to give clues about the sound of the last syllable, then if not solved give the second syllable or initial letter sound.

Level II

Follow the same as above but include the child's surname.

Rhyme game

(Sitting initially)

Each person in the group has a card from either of the word families. Give out cards depicting objects ending '*at*' or '*ouse*' (bat, cat, mouse), one to each person in the group. Help the children to identify the word linked to their picture then play the game by saying 'Stand up mouse, stand up bat, stand up cat, sit down mouse, stand up house, sit down bat' and so on.

Storylines

(Sitting)

In this session the aim is to encourage the use of a wider variety of verbs in addition to the positional words.

Lay out the bed, spider, mouse etc. in a ring in the middle of the circle. Remind the group about last week's session when they made up storylines using the spider, mouse, tree, table, bed and television. Talk about the actions they described, e.g. hiding under the table or the bed, up the tree. Extend to some new action words, e.g. jumping, crawling, tickling, hiding, climbing, sitting, lying. Ask them to close their eyes for a minute to try to remember what they saw. Encourage the children to use the new action words as they make up the storylines.

Ask a child to sit in the middle. One child at a time (adults join in too) tells the story and the child in the middle acts it out with the cards. Choose a good ending for the story.

Rhyme train

(Using the same visual prompt cards)

(Standing up in a circle)

Explain the game: 'This is my rhyme train. If your word sounds like mine, rhymes, then you can join my train when I ask you.'

Go around the circle showing and saying your word, e.g. 'Cat, will you join my sound train?' Help the children to decide if their word sounds like 'cat' and if so they join on your train behind you as you carry on round the circle.

Play the game using a word from the other family of words to include the other children.

Closing round: Pass a smile

(Standing)

Put on sad faces, then pass a smile round.

KS2 Session 15

MATERIALS NEEDED

- Responsive toy, or ball.
- Storyline cards: spider, bed, table, TV (in Appendix).
- Rhyming word cards (two sets).
- Two same-colour hoops; objects beginning with '*ch*' and '*f*'.
- Two cards, one with '*ch*' and one with '*f*', to go in the middle of the hoops.

Round

(Sitting)

1 Responsive toy, e.g. parrot (say name and wait for response).

Or

2 Roll the ball (saying 'I feel happy when...'), then roll the ball to someone else.

Storylines

(Sitting)

The aim in this session is to build on the work done in previous sessions. Remind the group about the stories they made up and the storylines they used. Talk about the actions the characters might do, e.g. hide, crawl, jump, tickle. Encourage the children to use these with positional words and nouns to produce

> Hiding under the table.
> Sitting on the bed.
> Crawling under the table.

Choose one child to sit in the middle and make up a story with help from the group. Ask children to close their eyes and remember some of the storylines they saw.

Rhyme train

(Using the same visual prompt cards)

(Standing up in a circle)

Explain the game: 'This is my rhyme train. If your word sounds like mine, rhymes, then you can join my train when I ask you.'

Go around the circle showing and saying your word, e.g. 'Cat, will you join my sound train?' Help the children to decide if their word sounds like 'cat' and if so they join on your train behind you as you carry on round the circle.

Play the game using a word from the other family of words to include the other children.

Sound hoops

(Using 'ch', 'f', or other selected sounds linked to the needs of the group. Standing up)

Put hoops down on the floor with the '*ch*' card in one and the '*f*' card in the other. Invite the children to select an object from the feely bag and guess what it is by feeling it, then take it out, identifying the initial sound. The child places the object in the correct sound hoop, with help and guidance as needed.

When all have had a turn, sit down and invite the children to remember who had what item and what it began with. Begin by asking each child what they had and what it began with. Then ask children if they can remember what particular children had.

Objects/pictures suggested

ch

cheese	chocolate
chain	chicken
Chewitts	chin

f

finger	foot
fork	fire
feather	football
farmer	

Closing game

(Standing)

Pass a smile and a handshake.

KS2 Session 16

Round

(Sitting)

1 With a responsive toy, e.g. a parrot, the child says his or her name and waits for a response.

Or

2 Roll the ball (saying 'I feel happy when . . .') then roll the ball to someone else.

Syllabilisation

mouse

hedgehog

butterfly

Lay out three cards, one with one syllable, one with two syllables, one with three syllables. Ponder about how many syllables/claps each has. An adult claps out the syllables, e.g.

hedge	hog
clap	clap

The children have to guess which card you are thinking of after several turns. Change the cards.

Fruit in the fridge

Stage I

Play one round of 'fruit box', where each child is identified with a fruit. Then play 'Sit down apples. Sit down pears. Stand up apples. Sit down bananas' and so on. (Check that all the children know which fruit they represent.)

Stage II

Explain that you are putting down one piece of card or hoop to be a fridge and one to be a cupboard. Then the children must listen carefully to see where they must go, cupboard or fridge, or back to the circle.

Call out

- Apples to the fridge.
- Bananas to the cupboard.
- Oranges to the fridge.
- Apples to the cupboard.
- Bananas to the circle.

Extend to give some problems to solve, e.g.

- Only two pears to the fridge and the other pears to the kitchen.
- Only one apple to the cupboard and the other apples to the fridge.
- The rest in the kitchen.

Storylines

(Sitting down)

Use a picture or model of a dragon or use visual cards if wished to recall sequence. Tell the children to close their eyes and picture what you are saying to them.

An adult tells the story of dragon who is in his cave and decides to go on holiday. He flies over trees and over a river, he sees sheep in the fields. He saw some caravans. He flew quietly up to the window and peeped in and he saw...

Take ideas from children. Use a blend of these ideas to continue story.

Pairwork

In pairs or threes talk about how the story will end.

Rhyming pairs

(Sitting)

The children pick from a feely bag with rhyming objects (two families, e.g. 'at' and 'in'). The children then find a partner with a rhyming card.

Close

Handshake.

MATERIALS NEEDED

- Ball.
- Bunch of jangly keys.
- Feely bag with rhyming object cards: '*at*', (cat, rat etc.), '*in*' (in, tin etc.).
- Playground picture from the Talkabout series from Black Sheep Press (tel: 01535 631346).

Round: roll the ball

(Sitting)

'My name is . . . and my favourite **circle game** is . . . ' Each child has one turn. Part of the task is to remember who has had a turn.

Question sheet

(Use the playground picture from the Talkabout series published by Black Sheep Press.)

1 Look together at the larger picture of children in the playground with one child, Bradley, standing on his own. Discuss ideas arising from it prompted by the questions to explore feelings and actions.
2 Present the four smaller pictures one at a time to generate discussion.
3 As a group decide on the best outcome for everyone.

Dragon's keys

(Sitting down)

Theme listening. You need a big jangly bunch of keys.
  Tell the dragon's story:

> Once there was a village where the people had lots of food to store but nowhere to put it. They asked the dragon who lived in a cave on the hill if they could put their food in his cave. He said 'Yes', he would lock it into his cave with his big bunch of keys. *[Show keys]*
>
>   But if he was asleep when the villagers came, he would get very cross if he was woken up and would roar. He suggested that if he was asleep, the villagers should try to take away the keys without waking him.

Explain that the dragon will sit in the middle of the circle with eyes closed and the keys beside him or her. Then a villager could try to take the keys away from the dragon without jangling them. If the dragon hears the keys, he wakes up and roars.

The dragon chooses the next dragon. The villager chooses the next villager by pointing when the dragon's eyes are closed.

Changing places

(Stand up to energise the group; keep very brief)

'I want to change places with . . .'

Rhyming pairs

(Sitting)

The children pick from a feely bag with rhyming objects. (two families, e.g. '*at*' and '*in*'). The children then find a partner with a rhyming card.

Sandwiches

(Sitting down)

'What is your favourite sandwich? Talk in pairs.' Take some ideas. See if they can remember each other's favourites.

Closing round

Shake hands and then pass a smile.

MATERIALS NEEDED

- Hand puppet.
- Three or four small pictures from Session 17 about the boy in the playground.
- Story picture of girl and spider (in Appendix p. 111).
- Question board (Toni's balloons). Colour code question circles.
- Cards showing pictures of mouse, hedgehog and butterfly (one, two, three syllables).
- Magic wand or stone.

Pass the sound

SSSSSSSSS

(Sitting down)

Pass an 's' sound from your mouth to your finger and on to the finger of the person next to you. The sound goes around to everyone. When it comes back to you 'put it back' on your lips and stop the sound. Pass 's' first. Pass 'f' next. *(Pass the sound as you would say it, not the letter name.)*

Puppets in the playground

(Recapping)

Reintroduce the hand puppet who is shy in the playground. Ask the children through the puppet what good ideas they had had last session when the little boy Bradley had no one to play with. (Lay out the three or four pictures from that session.) Talk about what would happen if he tried each idea.

The puppet thanks the children and is put away in his 'magic' box or cupboard.

Toni's balloons

Pin the picture from the Appendix (p. 114) on board or side of a box beside you so it can be easily seen by the group. Make sure it is enlarged to A3 at least.

Place the cut-out question circles (coloured) in front of you.

who? – blue
did what? – yellow
when? – red
where? – green
how? ⎫
why? ⎭ white

Tell the children that Toni wants lots of coloured balloons and that they are going to help by 'talking about what is happening in the picture'.

Distribute the picture of the girl and the spider (Appendix). Give each child a copy or share between two. Say this is today's picture story. Let the children look at the picture and discuss it in pairs. Ask them to tell you about the story. Accept what the children tell you and put the coloured balloons up with Blu-tack on the picture of Toni's balloons according to what they tell you.

For example, if they say 'girl drop cup', put up 'who' balloon (blue) and 'did what' (yellow) and give them lots of praise. Encourage them to look carefully to see if they can tell you 'When, Where, and Why?'

The idea is to elicit language details.

Syllabilisation

mouse

hedgehog

butterfly

Lay out three cards, one with one syllable, one with two syllables, one with three syllables. Ponder about how many syllables/claps each has. An adult claps out the syllables, e.g.

hedge   hog
clap   clap

The children have to guess which card you are thinking of after several turns. Change the cards.

Closing round

Pass round a wand or a 'wishing stone' and make a wish for myself.
Pass it round again and make a wish for someone else.

MAGIC

82

KS2 Session 19

Round

Each person claps their name round the circle, e.g. Pat-rick (clap clap), John (clap)

Storylines

(Sitting down)

Encourage the children to **close their eyes to aid their memory.** Recap on the things the dragon did when you first told this story in Session 16. Use a picture or model of dragon or use visual cards if wished to recall the sequence.

An adult tells the story of the dragon who is in his cave and decides to go on holiday. He flies over trees and over a river, he sees sheep in the fields. He saw some caravans. He flew quietly up to the window and peeped in and he saw...

Take ideas from the children. Use a blend of these ideas to continue the story. See if the children can think of different storylines. Encourage a definite *end* to the story.

Mr Bear's honeypot

(Sitting down)

(To remind about question categories; living creatures)

Play once.

Tell a story of a bear who likes to play a game with the animals in the forest by hiding something in his pot. The group ask Mr Bear questions and Mr Bear answers them. When someone guesses the object correctly Mr Bear shows the group what is in the pot. *(Use Mr Bear as a puppet. The children ask him directly and he answers them.)*

Hide a creature

Hide a creature first (animal, bird, insect, reptile). Place the 'question cards' in the middle of the circle. They are:

> Where does it live?
> How does it move?
> Is it a living creature?
> What does it have on its body?
> What colour is it?

Choose a symbol to add to each question to aid recognition, e.g. a house on the 'Where does it live?' card.

Tell the children what the questions are, and to talk in **pairs**. Pairs pick up a question card each. Go round the circle encouraging them to answer the question on their card (prompt: read them out for them if necessary). Put the card by the pot when it has been used.

At the end of this, recap on the answers, e.g. 'Mmm, we found out it is a living creature, it has no legs, it has scales on its body and it slithers. What could it be? What do you think it is?'

Dragon's wink

(Standing up; energising)

A child chosen to be the dragon crosses the circle and winks at one person and changes places. That person then goes over to someone else and winks and so on.

Feeling worried

(Sitting up)

Puppet animal tells how he is not feeling happy. He is worried. Show a large picture of a worried child. Talk about a time when you were worried.

Show the sheet from Pragmatic pictures with eight small pictures, four of which show situations which could be worrying *(21, 22, 23, 24: lost dog, broken window, late for school, lost homework)*. Give a slow verbal description of what is happening in each one of the four, then ask children for their ideas as to which one would be most worrying.

Puppet at the end decides what had worried him.

Circle train

(To focus the group; standing up)

Choose a child as the engine. This child chooses others, saying 'Will you join my sound train?'

Closing round: Pass a smile

(Standing)

Put on sad faces then pass a smile round.

KS2 Session 20

Round: name point game

Tell the children, 'Point to another person in the circle and say *your own name*.' Point out it is hard to do . . . get faster.

Dragon's keys

(Sitting down)

Theme listening. You need a big jangly bunch of keys.

  Tell the dragon's story:

> Once there was a village where the people had lots of food to store but nowhere to put it. They asked the dragon who lived in a cave on the hill if they could put their food in his cave. He said 'Yes', he would lock it into his cave with his big bunch of keys. *[Show keys.]*
>   But if he was asleep when the villagers came, he would get very cross if he was woken up and would roar. He suggested that if he was asleep, the villagers should try to take away the keys without waking him.

Explain that the dragon will sit in the middle of the circle with eyes closed and the keys beside him or her. Then a villager could try to take the keys away from the dragon without jangling them. If the dragon hears the keys, he wakes up and roars.
  The dragon chooses the next dragon. The villager chooses the next villager by pointing when the dragon's eyes are closed.

What we say in the playground

(Sitting)

Using the large picture of the playground scene, recap on the ideas from Session 18, when Bradley was on his own in the playground. Ask if anything like this has ever happened to them.
  Invite children either to use puppets to role play one of these situations *or* to use masks (choose masks that allow them to see and speak clearly, e.g. half-masks or stick-supported masks).

Rhyme cards

Pass a feely bag containing pictures of objects in the '*at*' and '*an*' families of words.

cat	van
mat	pan
rat	can
bat	man

Each person chooses one. Go round the circle identifying each one.
Lay out large pieces of card (same colour and size).

> *Choose one 'at' person to stand on one.*
> *Choose one 'an' person to stand on the other.*

Their test is to call people to join them if they have the same sound card. **'Ashley, will you come with me?' 'Yes [no] I will [can't]. I have an at [an] card.'** Talk about the rhymes.

Sit in the circle again. Sit two children in the middle. Randomly assign cards. Allow them to play 'snap' while the group watch. They say the name of the object as they put it down. Gather in the cards.

Pass the pretend rhyme box

(Sitting down)

'I have a [word] in my box.' This can be previously discussed with the group in terms of the sound of the word and words which would rhyme with it. Each person in the circle takes the imaginary box and says 'I have a [rhyming word] in my box.' This can be used to check how well the group remember the words used in the previous game.

Closing round

'My name is and I like...'

KS2 Session 21

Round

Pass a tambourine or bells round as quietly as you can. The leader calls out *behind* or *in front* or *shake* and the person holding it has to follow that instruction.

Storylines

(Adding speech)

(Sitting down)

Use the spider, cat, tree, chair, house and bed laid down in the circle. One person in the middle of the circle moves the pieces. Each person in the circle takes turns to say what they think happened (*action*).

- Ask what the spider/teddy/girl felt (*feelings*).
- Ask 'What did the spider/teddy/girl say when that happened?' (*spoken outcome*).

Do this several times.

Guess the name

Level I

An adult claps the first name of a child without saying it. The task of the group is to guess whose name it is. For example, if the name is 'Robin' talk about it having two syllables or claps. Some children have names with one syllable or clap, so it can't be their name. Some children have three syllables or claps so it can't be them. If the children cannot work it out begin to give clues about the sound of the last syllable, then if not solved give the second syllable or initial letter sound.

Level II (optional)

Follow the same procedure as above but include the child's surname.

Rhyme game

(Sitting initially)

Each person in the group has a card from either of the word families. Give out cards depicting objects ending '*at*' or '*ouse*' (bat, cat, mouse), one to each person in the group. Help the children to identify the word linked to their picture then play the game by saying 'Stand up mouse, stand up bat, stand up cat, sit down mouse, stand up house, sit down bat' and so on. Then 'Mouse find a rhyming partner', 'Bat find a rhyming partner', 'House find a new rhyming partner'.

Rhyme train

(Using the same visual prompt cards)

(Standing up in a circle)

Explain the game: 'This is my rhyme train. If your word sounds like mine, rhymes, then you can join my train when I ask you.'

Go around the circle showing and saying your word, e.g. 'Cat, will you join my sound train?' Help the children to decide if their word sounds like 'cat' and, if so, they join on to your train behind you as you carry on round the circle.

Play the game using a word from the other family of words to include the other children.

Dragon's wink

(Standing up; energising)

A child chosen to be the dragon crosses the circle and winks at one person and changes places. That person then goes over to someone else and winks and so on.

Closing round

Pass a wink and a smile.

KS2 Session 22

Round

Pass a picture of a happy person. Each person says he or she is happy because...

Name point game

(Standing)

Say to the children, 'Point to someone else in the circle and say your own name.' Talk about how hard it is to point to someone and say your name, not theirs.

Talkabout

(Sitting)

Use question sheet 2. Show the picture of the little boy displaying his drawing. Talk about the reasons why the teacher or the children might laugh. **Positive:** Fun, liking the fun in the picture, because they want the boy to feel happy. **Negative:** Spite, not being kind.

Look at the four smaller pictures one by one and use the questions as prompts to decide which would be the best solution all round.

Rhyme train

(Without using the same visual prompt cards)

(Standing up in a circle)

Explain the game: 'This is my rhyme train. If your word sounds like mine, rhymes, then you can join my train when I ask you.'

Go around the circle showing and saying your word, e.g. 'Cat, will you join my sound train?' Help the children to decide if their word sounds like 'cat' and, if so, they join on to your train behind you as you carry on round the circle.

Play the game using a word from the other family of words to include the other children.

Syllabilisation

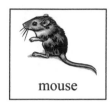
mouse

hedgehog

butterfly

Lay out three cards, one with one syllable, one with two syllables, one with three syllables. Ponder about how many syllables/claps each has. An adult claps out the syllables (next time this will be extended to four syllables).

hedge   hog
clap   clap

The children have to guess which card you are thinking of after several turns. Change the cards.

Closing round

Pass round a 'wishing stone' and make a wish for someone else.

MAGIC

Round

Tell the children, 'Say your name to the parrot' or 'Pass the object across the circle. When you have the object you say 'My favourite toy is...'

Dozy Dog and Annie have an adventure: you decide

(Sitting)

Use props of trees and houses and, for example, a tiger. Tell the story of Dozy Dog and Annie going for a walk in the village.

Sit one child in the middle of the circle with the props. Take ideas from around the circle:

- What happens to Dozy Dog and Annie? The child in the middle shows the props accordingly to make a little play.
- What do they both feel? Show the four pictures of Annie in different moods.
- How do we want the story to end?
- Encourage all the children to close their eyes and think of the storyline and the ending and how they feel.

Dragon's wink

(Standing up; energising)

A child chosen to be the dragon crosses the circle and winks at one person and changes places. That person then goes over to someone else and winks and so on.

Bored

Puppet tells the group that he is feeling bored today. Take ideas from the group as to what could have happened to him, e.g.

- Shopping with mum.
- Wet play.
- Waiting for an adult.
- TV breaks.

Talk about mixed emotions, e.g. bored and angry, bored and scared. Talk about what they could do or think about to help them. Show three faces to choose from. Which one shows the boy feeling bored?

Rhyme train

(Using different words and visual prompt cards)

(Standing up in a circle)

Explain the game: 'This is my rhyme train. If your word sounds like mine, rhymes, then you can join my train when I ask you.'

Go around the circle showing and saying your word, e.g. 'Cat, will you join my sound train?' Help the children to decide if their word sounds like 'cat' and, if so, they join on your train behind you as you carry on round the circle.

Play the game using a word from the other family of words to include the other children.

Sound hoops

(Using 'ch', 'sh', or other selected sounds linked to the needs of the group. Standing up)

Put hoops down on the floor with a *'ch'* card and a *'sh'* card in them. Invite the children to select an object from the feely bag and guess what it is by feeling it then take it out, identifying the initial sound. The child places the object in the correct sound hoop, with help and guidance as needed.

When all have had a turn, sit down and invite the children to remember who had what item and what it began with. Begin by asking each child what they had and what it began with. Then ask children if they can remember what particular children had.

Objects/pictures suggested

ch		**sh**	
cheese	chocolate	shell	shape
chain	chicken	ship	sheep
Chewitts	chin	shirt	sugar (to raise discussion)
		shoe	

Closing game

(Standing)

Pass a smile.

KS2 Session 24

Round

(Sitting)

Pass an object to each other across the circle, asking 'Are you happy today?' The person receiving the object answers, 'Yes' or 'No' and then asks the next person 'Are you happy today?'

Syllabilisation

Lay out four cards with pictures of one-, two-, three- and four-syllable words, e.g. house, hedgehog, dinosaur, supermarket.

house

hedgehog

dinosaur

supermarket

Ponder about how many syllables/claps each has. An adult claps out the syllables, e.g.

hedge	hog
clap	clap

The children have to guess which card you are thinking of after several turns. Change the cards.

Mr Bear's honeypot and question cards: extending to a new set

(Sitting down)

(To remind about question categories)

Play once.

Tell a story of a bear who likes to play a game with the animals in the forest by hiding something in his pot. The group ask Mr Bear questions and Mr Bear answers them. When someone guesses the object correctly Mr Bear shows the group what is in the pot. *(Use Mr Bear as a puppet. The children ask him directly and he answers them.)*

Hide an object to do with transport

Hide an object first (e.g. car, tractor, aeroplane, helicopter, boat, motorbike). Place the 'question cards' in the middle of the circle. They are:

> Does it have wheels?
> Where is it kept at night?
> Does it travel along the ground?
> Does it have an engine?
> How many people can it hold?

(Choose a symbol to add to each question to aid recognition, e.g. a garage on the 'Where is it kept at night?' card.

Tell the children what the questions are. Tell them to talk in **pairs**. Pairs pick up a question card each. Go round the circle encouraging them to ask their questions on their card (prompt: read them out for them if necessary).

At the end of this recap on the answers, e.g. 'Mmm, we found out it has wheels, it is kept in a garage at night, it has an engine, and three or four people can go in it. What could it be? What do you think it is?'

I'm worried, what can I do?

Show the picture of a worried child. Remind the children of the session when we looked at the four worrying situations – lost dog, broken window, lost homework, late for school.

Talk about a time when you were worried. Ask around the group for their experiences. Choose one experience and get ideas on what might have helped the person, ideas they could have tried.

Closing round

(Standing)

I'm happy when...

Appendix: photocopiables

Mr Bear's Question Cards

Does it
have wheels?

Where is it
kept at night?

Does it travel along
the ground?

Does it have
an engine?

How many people
can it hold?

Mr Bear's Question Cards

Where does it live?

How does it move?

How many legs?

What does it have on its body?

What colour is it?

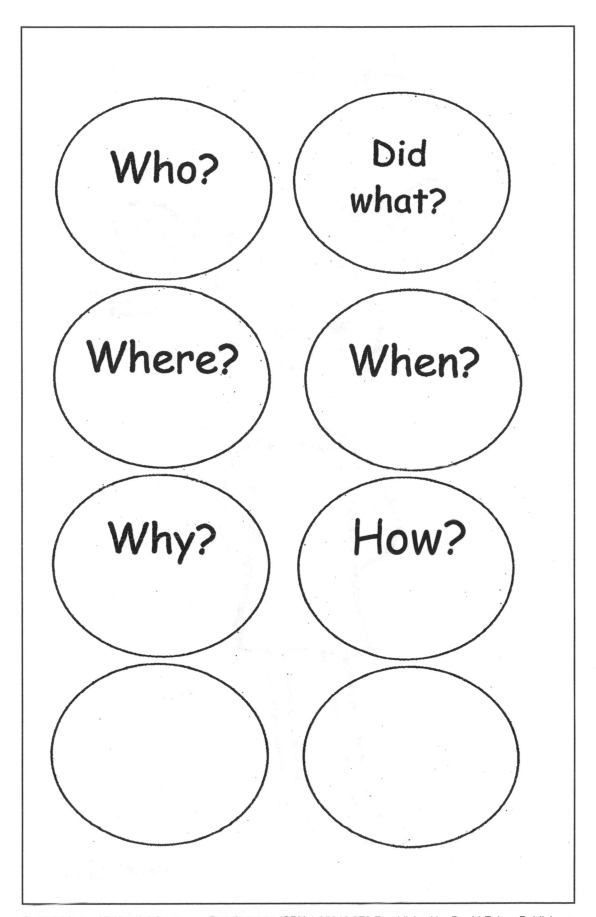

Annie

Heidi Lowe

Heidi Lowe

Heidi Lowe

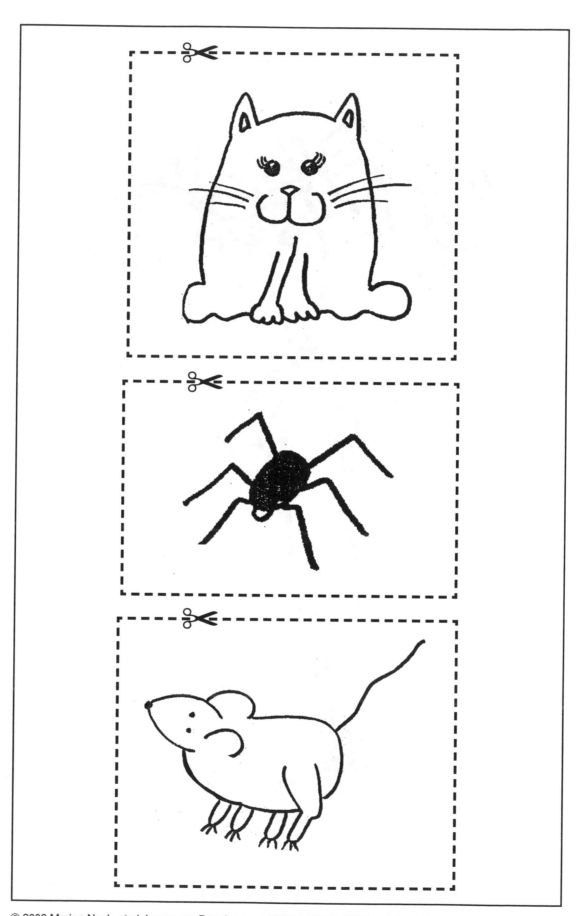

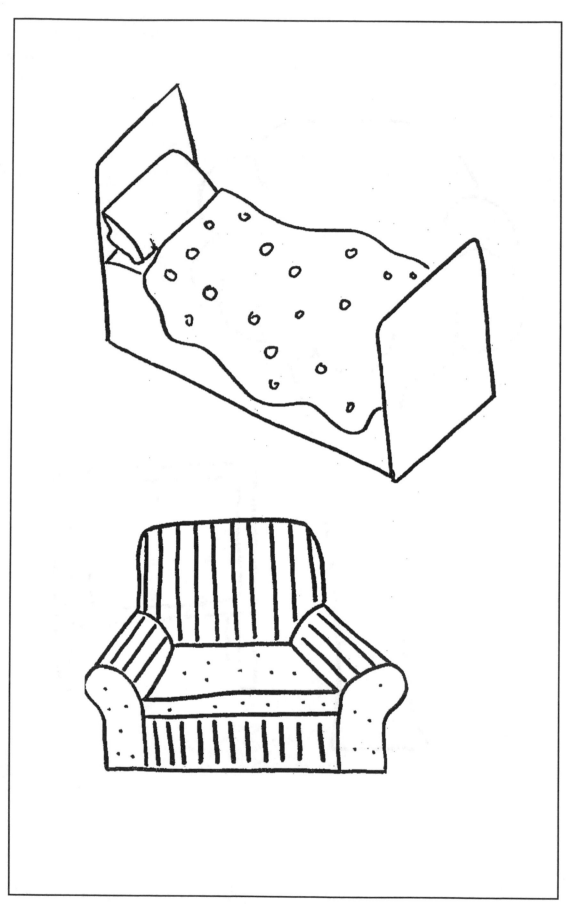

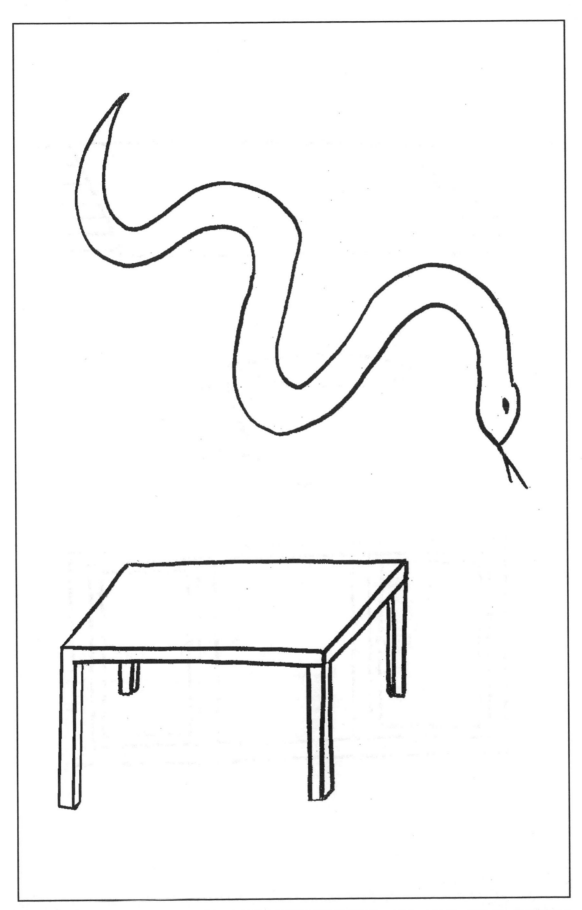

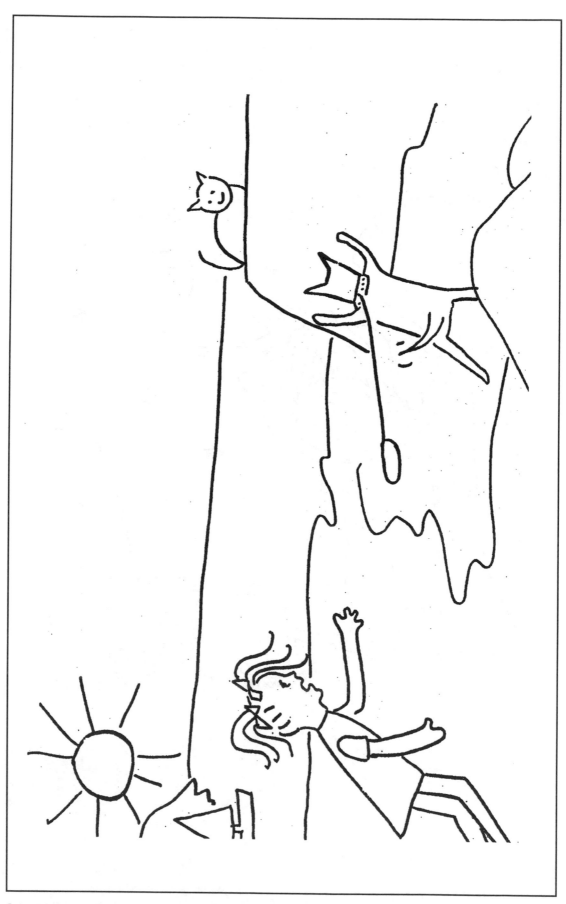